IGNORED
OR
ILL-REPRESENTED?

The Grievance of Terai-Madhes Conflict in Nepal

IGNORED OR ILL-REPRESENTED?

The Grievance of Terai-Madhes Conflict in Nepal

Bishnu Raj Upreti
Suman Babu Paudel
Safal Ghimire

ADROIT

Adroit Publishers
New Delhi

Published by

ADROIT PUBLISHERS

4675/21, Ganpati Bhawan, Ansari Road,
Daryaganj, New Delhi-110 002

Phone : 011-23266030

Distributors

AKHIL BOOK DISTRIBUTORS

email: akhilbooks@yahoo.com
akhilbks@gmail.com

Cover photo: Bijay Rai/NCCR North-South

ISBN : 978-81-87392-99-6

Printed in India on behalf of M/s Adroit Publishers by
Akhil Sharma, E-mail: adroitpublishers@gmail.com

Dedicated to those who suffered from years of exclusion, brought about historical changes always deserve justice and are promoting fraternity for an integrated and egalitarian Nepal

Preface and Acknowledgements

In the wake of recent democratic movements in Nepal, Terai-Madhes region has emerged as a hot topic in Nepalese politics and academia. It is now known not only as an agriculturally fertile, but also a politically contested and a militarily insecure region. There is a contest for recognition, for representation, for approach to tackle security problems created by the rise of 109 armed groups and for redistribution of power to over tens of ethnic groups residing in this region. Let the remaining other issues, there is also a contest for the name of the region itself. Among the people, some prefer to be known as Madhesis, some others prefer to be called as Teraivasis. Whatever the present contentions are, the people in this region had long been commonly suffering from the ignorance by the establishment and regional elites in terms of esteem, identity, recognition and redistribution.

In this context, the book talks about some pertinent issues on Terai-Madhes. It begins its journey from the semantic debate on the region, illustrates the historical context of exclusion and discrimination, provides a snapshot of the popular uprising of 2007 and explores the causes behind the prolonged conflict. Mainly focusing on the rise of communalism in this region and its severe impacts, it also details positive and negative impacts of the overall conflict in Terai-Madhes region.

Nepal has always been a geo-political hub for international powerhouses, so has been the Terai-Madhes once its domestic political and military importance rose higher after 2007. So, this book also examines the interest of India, China and some other western countries over this issue.

In the new socio-political context of post-2007 Terai-Madhes, academic studies could have analysed the issues and offered best solutions. Sadly, such studies are very few in this critical political phase in Nepal. Often, the literature available on Terai-Madhes is partisan or advocacy-oriented or merely anthropological. Further, the lack of authentic data and the absence of comprehensive analysis from broader transformation perspective are misguiding a proper understanding of the dynamics of Terai-Madhes conflict. The problems found in the existing publications are that they advance arguments treating 'Terai-Madhes' as one homogenous region. They fail to analyse the gender, caste, ethnic and cultural variations as well as inequities within this region. Of course, Terai-Madhes and the people here had been suffering from marginalisation by the state since long. But to transform its conflict, there needs a scientific scrutiny to properly locate the causes and apply the solutions. Merely this book may not be sufficient to do so but it brings issues and concerns to be further analysed. Hence, there needs rigorous researches from intelligentsia on these issues in future.

There are many people behind the curtain who made possible for this book to come into its present shape. To name few of them, we are sincerely thankful for the intellectual company of Dr Anita Ghimire, Dr Purna Nepali, Rajya Laxmi Gurung, Tulasi Sharan Sigdel and Sony KC. We also sincerely acknowledge the hard-work from Gp Acharya on extracting information to elaborate the contents. South Asia Regional Support Officer of NCCR North-South, Siddhi Manandhar, has been very supportive to us as always on logistic matters.

We acknowledge support from the Swiss National Centre of Competence in Research (NCCR) North-South, co-funded by the Swiss National Science Foundation (SNSF), the Swiss Agency for Development and Cooperation (SDC) and the participating institutions as this research is an academic product of this collaboration.

Unforgettably, Adroit Publishers deserves our best thank for its esteemed consideration to this book by agreeing to publish it. We are sincerely grateful to our respondents during the research whose information and insights helped us craft our perspectives with better evidence. Last but not the least, we request our valuable readers, to whom we are much obliged for their time to go through this book, to provide us creative comments and suggestions that help us work more and do better.

With sincere thanks,

The Authors

April 2012

CONTENTS

List of Tables

List of Figures

Abbreviations and Acronyms

ACHR	Asian Centre for Human Rights
AK-47	Avtomat Kalashnikova 1947
APF	Armed Police Force
CA	Constituent Assembly
CBES	Chure Bhawar Ekata Samaj
CBS	Central Bureau of Statistics
CDO	Chief District Officer
CPA	Comprehensive Peace Agreement
CPN-UML	Communist Party of Nepal- Unified Marxist and Leninist
DDC	District Development Committe
EC	Election Commission
GDP	Gross Domestic Product
ICG	International Crisis Group
INSEC	Informal Sector Service Centre
JTMM	Janatantrik Terai Mukti Morcha
JTMM-J	Janatantrik Terai Mukti Morcha-Jwala
JTMM-G	Janatantrik Terai Mukti Morcha- Goit
MNLF	Madhesi National Liberation Front
MPRF	Madhesi People's Right Forum
MPRF-D	Madhesi People's Right Forum-Democratic
NC	Nepali Congress

NSP	Nepal Sadvawana Party
SSS	Special Security Strategy
SLR	Self Loading Rifle
SMG	Sub-Machine Gun
SPA	Seven Party Alliance
SRC	State Restructuring Commission
TMDP	Terai Madhes Democratic Party
UCPN (M)	United Communist Party of Nepal (Maoist)
UDMF	United Democratic Madhesi Front
UN	United Nations
UNMIN	United Nations Mission in Nepal
VDC	Village Development Committee

1

INTRODUCTION TO TERAI-MADHES

In Nepal's history, Terai-Madhes[1], the southern plain land, used to identify itself as an agricultural and industrial area. But sarcastically, the same people living in this area have been feeling it as a politically marginalised and manipulated geography. This region, previously known as the 'bread basket' of the country, changed into an icon as a 'violent zone' of Nepal. Even during the Maoist insurgency (1996-2006), this region was comparatively peaceful than hill regions (ICG 2003) and (INSEC 2007). Population density was low until 1960s, the time when the government declared it as Malaria-free region. However, the population expanded after this declaration. This socio-economically fertile region fell into a serious contention immediately after the Comprehensive Peace Agreement (CPA) between the United Communist Party of Nepal (UCPN-Maoist)[2] and the Government of Nepal in 2006. Terai-Madhes expressed its dissatisfaction through racially politicised regional uprising in 2007. Following this, the region became an uncertain, insecure and a conflict-ridden zone as the hill-origin people living in the region became the deliberate targets after the communal violence in the aftermath of the uprising. The peace and consanguinity that existed before remain unrecovered yet.

The contention on some of the critical issues had already surfaced after the 1990's political change. It was more visible this time. Then, the leaders of Terai-Madhes started to show their dissatisfaction capitalising some sensitive issues such as access to citizenship certificate, electoral representation and distribution of power and economic resources. Similarly, marginalisation of languages and customary rights of the people were other concerns. The state's attention to these issues was insufficient until the Terai-Madhes awoke in the 2007 uprising. After this, not only the political issues, but also the socio-economy of this region appeared as a matter of study, analysis and discussion. In this context, this book reflects on the conflict, security and communal relation in the region. Further, the chapters here also contemplate on some of the major causes behind this conflict, its effects, and international interests over it.

Figure 1 Map of Nepal with Terai-Madhes Region in Highlight

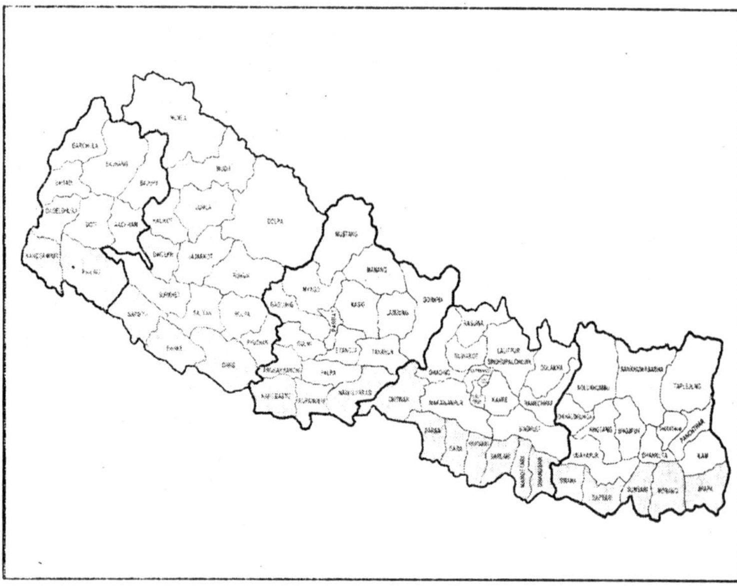

Source: Designed by the authors

1.1 The semantic debate

The geographic definition of Terai-Madhes is highly contested as Tharu indigenous organisations from the same region do not agree with the term 'Madhes'. They rather highlight and emphasise the term 'Terai' (Chaudhary 2007). Several other researchers, historians and politicians have also questioned on the naming of 'Terai' as 'Madhes'. But other people known as 'Madhesi' do not accept the term 'Terai' and choose the term 'Madhes'. To manage this contention, the decision-makers came to a negotiated settlement by naming the region as 'Terai-Madhes'. It stretches from east to west as part of the Indo-Gangetic Plain (ICG 2007). Twenty districts of Nepal (Jhapa, Morang, Sunsari, Saptari, Siraha, Dhanusha, Mahottari, Sarlahi, Bara, Parsa, Rautahat, Chitwan, Kapilvastu, Kailali, Kanchanpur, Bardiya, Banke, Dang, Rupandehi and Nawalparasi) fall under the region.

The politicians and scholars in Nepal still debate on whether to call the southern plain of Nepal 'Madhes' or 'Terai'. The conceptual difference is strong. Chaudhary (2007) argues that the word 'Madhes' is originated from 'Madhyadesh'. He states that the Madhyadesh was at the central region ('Madhya' meaning 'centre' and 'Desh' meaning 'the region' in Sanskrit) of India so it was called 'Madhyadesh'. Nepal was never under the control of India. So, Chaudhary argues that Nepal's 'Terai' was never the 'Madhyadesh'. Unlike him, the scholars claiming the word 'Madhes' are raising long historical background dating back to the kingdom of Videha or Mithila (Yadav 2006b and Yadav 2007). Nayak (2011) views the area between hills and the Indian Plain as Madhyadesh or Madhes. Gupta (2010) also argues that 'Madhes' is the land which has been renamed as 'Terai'. Madhesis, as he defines, are the son of the Madhes land (Dhartiputra). Others argue that Dhartiputra are only the Tharus and all the others are the immigrants from the south (Chaudhary 2007, Pradhan and Shrestha 2005). Therefore, debates are still going on showing the need for further exploration.

Oxford dictionary explains 'Terai' as a belt of wet jungle lying between the lower foothills of the Himalayas and the plains.

However, indigenous Tharus claim that the word Terai was derived from 'Tar' meaning 'low', the characteristic of the plain region (Cheah 2008). These all definitions of Terai seem close to each other, although, at present context, the term 'Terai-Madhes' refers geographically to the lowland along Nepal's border with India (ICG 2007).

Giving diverse opinion on the history of this plain land, Shah (2006), Yadav (2006b) and Gupta (2010) state the history of Madhes has still been veiled and suspicious. They claim that this region's issue and history are overshadowed because of the ignorance of the Pahadi (People of hill origin) scholars and historians who dominated the academia. On the other side, Neupane (2005) argues that, even in the history of Nepal, Madhes has not been explained well because of the dense forest and less human settlements in that region. One cannot negate the fact that the issues of this region were in shadows because of the insignificant effort of local scholars to bring them into public debate (Burkert 1997). The focus of such writers was not on social sciences to raise Madhesi issues. The local scholars focused much on explanatory arts, culture, language, literature, physical science, mathematics and other technical subjects (Dahal 2005 as cited in Hachhethu 2007).

Interestingly, Chaudhary (2007) has denied the presence of Madhes land in Nepal's territory. He accepts that Madhesis are in Nepal but Madhyadesh was never in Nepal. He argues that the word 'Madhes' has conspiringly replaced the word 'Terai'; all the people who call themselves Madhesi are the Indian migrants from 'Madhyadesh'. He argues that the indigenous people such as Tharus are the only original inhabitants of Terai. Gaige (2009) has also backed the arguments of Chaudhary (2007) stating that non-Hindu castes such as Tharus are the original inhabitants of Terai region. He argues that the other Hindus and Muslims in the plain are migrants into the Terai or the descendants of those migrants. Neupane (2005) also believes that Madhyadesh was formed in Indian Territory. He adds that when Hindu Brahmins chased

Buddhists from the plain of Ganga[3] and Yamuna[4]; the Brahmins then gave the name Madhyadesh to the plain from Ambala[5] to Prayag[6]. Later, it was called Madhayadesh. Pradhan and Shrestha (2005) have seconded the idea that the Madhesis are migrants. They posit that a large number of Maithili speaking people came across the border for job and business. Later, they settled in Terai. Gaige (2009) explains that the first plain caste people, settled in Terai region were Ahirs (Yadavs) and cowherds who used to come seasonally (from October to January) for grazing. Subsequently they made these places their permanent residence. Other groups including Muslims came following them. Tharus allege that the same group has now been claiming of being the son of the land.[7] Pathak and Uprety (2009) also describe Madhesis as the new immigrants from India. Madhesi political leaders and scholars are not ready to accept these arguments. So, Tharus are strongly insisting to call the region as 'Terai'; whereas Madhesis are enforcing to use the term 'Madhes'. On this debate, the Maoist government came on political negotiation terming this region as Terai-Madhes.

Addressing the uprising, the government made the first amendment in the Interim Constitution-2007 and used the term 'Madhes' to name the region.[8] Concerning that amendment, Tharus protested heavily insisting to use the word 'Terai' in place of 'Madhes'. Later, addressing the wills of both Tharus and Madhesis, the government became ready to use the word 'Terai-Madhes' so that none of the communities would feel discriminated of their identity.[9] Yet, Tharus and Madhesis are holding their demand tightly so far.

1.2 Defining Madhesi and Non-Madhesi

Defining the terms 'Madhes' and 'Madhesi' is a difficult job; it is simply because of their controversy in Nepalese politics at present. Terai-Madhes covers significant proportion of the Shiwalik hill region (Shah 2006). Hachhethu (2007) argues that there is 36 per cent hill-origin population in Terai-Madhes. If this all southern plain is defined geographically as 'Madhes', every people including hill-origin people as well as Tharus (who themselves claim as non-Madhesi) in that region should be called 'Madhesis'. But Madhesi leaders interpret 'Madhes' more ethnically than geographically. Some analysts such as Dahal (1996), Hachhethu (2007) and Yadav (2006b) have defined Madhesis as the people originated in this plain region except those originated from the hill, which is a frequently contested argument.

Gellener (1997) has used the word 'Madhesi' to refer to the people of Indian origin in the southern plain of Nepal. Nayak (2011) has a different term. He has used the term 'Indian Madhesis' to refer to the people of Indian origin (who are at present called as Madhesis). Even some early writings of C. K. Lal admit that the Indian migrants are called as Madhesi in Nepal. He writes that in twentieth century, there was heavy starvation in Indian states Bihar, Bengal and Uttar Pradesh. In the mean time, there was heavy deforestation in the Nepalese southern plain. Many Indians came and settled here that time. They were later called as Madhesis because they were from Madhes.[10]

No matter whatever definition different scholars have, one should admit the fact that there is much dissimilarity among them while categorising 'Madhesi' community. The population in Terai-Madhes is composed of altogether 59 ethnic and caste groups (Jha 2010) making this categorisation a complex job. Dahal (1996) has divided Madhesi community into four groups:

a) indigenous Janajatis (ethnic people) living in Madhes for generations,
b) people belonging with traditional Hindu caste hierarchy,
c) businesspersons of Indian origin e.g. Marwadi, Sikh and others, and
d) Muslims.

For Hachhethu (2007), there are three distinct cultural groups: plain's Hindu caste, plain's Janajatis group and Muslims. Studies such as Shah (2006), Hachhethu (2007) and Dahal (1996) have included all communities except hill origin people into one Madhesi (plain people) category. Apart from them, Nayak (2011) has divided Madhesi population into three communities:

a) Indigenous people,

b) Pahadi Madhesis (hill-origin people in Terai-Madhes), and

c) Indian Madhesis.

Indeed, most of the people advocating for Madhesi rights are faultily claiming only non-hill-origin people as Madhesis. Some scholars have also used term 'ethnic Madhesis' for the Indian-origin people in this region. But Muslims, Sikhs and other indigenous nationalities who do not belong to caste hierarchy are also included as Madhesis (terming as 'Madhesi cultural group') by Yadav (2007), Hachhethu (2007) and Dahal (1996). These scholars have defined 'Madhesi' group only geographically, an approach that Muslims and Tharu indigenous people are defying. Further, their analyses excluded the hill-origin people residing for generations in the plain land, which seems to become a source of tension and potential precursor for ethnic violence in the region.

There is cultural and religious difference within the people categorised as 'Madhesis'. But, in the changing political context, Muslims do not want to be called just as 'Madhesis'. They were calling themselves as Madhesis before and during Madhes uprising. They equally participated in Madhes uprising; some of them became martyrs too. But now they are demanding their separate identity more than just being recognised as the Madhesis.[11] It is natural that the religious minorities, Muslims, do not want to be identified just as Madhesis, the geographic minorities. There are two reasons: first, there may be the possibility of elite capture from religious majorities in opportunities; second, Muslmis in Nepal live not only in Terai-Madhes, but also in hill areas. The growth rate of Muslims population is very high in hills. If we look at the census report of 1981-2001, Doti, Surkhet and Dhading districts alone have the growth rate of 176.8 per cent, 54.4 per cent and 54.1 per cent respectively in terms of Muslim population.

The growth rate of Muslims there is greater than the growth rate of the total population of the district (Satyal 2003).

Tharu indigenous group also strongly denies calling them as Madhesis, except some Tharus in the eastern part (ICG 2007). Tharus are claiming themselves as the original inhabitants of the region and the remaining dwellers as migrants. Along Tharus, there are also other ethnic groups, who now want separate identities than just being called as Madhesi. Only including them within Madhesi might not secure their separate and unique identities. Contrary to it, Yadav (2007) and some other writers with similar analysis claim all except hill-origin people in the region as Madhesis collectively. Regarding some Tharus in the east, Neupane (2005), referring to Acharya (1997), writes that Aryans of plain used to keep the Kirat Tharus and Dhimal in their society as the slaves. Later, plain Aryans left making them slaves and they began to freely reside in the same region. This way, Kirats, Tharus, Mongols and Dhimals slowly left their culture and assimilated Aryan life-styles behaving as Madhesi Janajatis.

To clarify the identity issue and to provide reservations in services, government had tried to define the term 'Madhesi'. It listed 92 caste groups[12] including Tharus as Madhesi in reservation ordinance in 2009.[13] But Tharus have been withdrawn from the list after their heavy protest. According to the government provision, if there is confusion on identifying someone as Madhesi, it would be distinguished from their physical features and mother-tongue. The state gave authority to Chief District Officers (CDOs) to distinguish Madhesis and non Madhesis. Due to this, it came on controversy as CDOs could misuse authority. Some cases of controversy also came when hill-origin people born and residing in Madhes passed the Public Service Commission exams in reservation quotas being identified as Madhesis. Madhesi activists and politicians highly criticised this trend. So this definition could not hold strong ground after falling under sharp controversy. Some Madhesi Dalits, indigenous nationalities and backward people protested against the state that imposed Madhesi identity on them.

They wanted their different identity within the Madhesi.[14] There is fear that their privileges could be snatched by the class and caste elites from within the Madhesi reservation quota. Muslims have the same case as Tharus do. The fourth amendment of the Interim Constitution-2007 has listed Muslims under the Madhesi category. But Muslim group has strong disagreement over it. In 2010, the United Muslims National Struggle Committee announced protest programs demanding their separate religious identity.[15] Responding to it, the government classified them under the 'Terai' group (Pathak and Uprety 2009). Due to frequent protests from different caste and ethnic organisations, the cabinet meeting on 4 March 2009 decided to finalise the list of Madhesis only after holding consultation with the concerned organisations of indigenous nationalities. Alike the Tharus and Muslims there are many other ethnic groups that participated in the uprising in 2007 are seeking separate identity than Madhesi. Different groups of people irrespective of origin, caste and religion participated in the uprising. Their commonality was the marginalisation by the state. Now, the different groups are claiming for a special identity and self-determination[16] (Cheah 2008). Now, the identity politics, manipulated by different vested interests, has not only created tension and disrupted communal harmony but also seriously devided the people in to ethnic line.

Government effort to categorise Madhesi caste groups has been insignificant compared to the discontent over this issue. Regarding the lack of concrete definition of Madhesi, Tharu activist Satya Mohan Joshi (Tharu) argued that there is no legal definition for Madhesi. The government should be clear about who Madhesi are. Only then the real Madhesis could benefit from the reservation system. The state, first of all, should be crystal clear about differences between Madhesi and indigenous nationalities. There should be some definitive laws in this regard. Those who have separate identity should not be called only Madhesis collectively. It could be a reason for the loss of their speciality.[17]

Since the people in Terai-Madhes have varieties of origin, it is always controversial to state the all people living there as Madhesis.

A question emerges here on why and how Madhesi identity became so strong? Marginalisation and exclusion from the capital-centreed government made people here unite in a single cluster as Madhesis. Different ethnic, class, caste, religious and cultural groups united in this regional identity. The exclusive behaviour and marginalisation was the only common thing among the people in Terai-Madhes. It brought them close to each other and bound as Madhesis (Chaudhary 2007; Cheah 2008 and Nayak 2011). Since, the state itself began responding to them with pan-Madhesis, this common image slowly became their strength. Acharya (1997) as cited in Neupane (2005) argues that Nepalis, especially hill-origin ones, started to call Madhes not only to that Indian plain area (Madhya Desh) but also to this Nepalese southern plain. In this way, the word 'Madhes' became a synonym of Terai and the people of that region became Madhesis. In this way, the group which is called as Madhesis does not have a homogenous identity; it is a cluster of different cultural, religious and ethnic groups residing in the same region. So, the way of addressing all people in that region as Madhesis has been taken by the other natives as an imposition of the identity of 'Migrant Madhesis' and is described as an unjust practice.

Tharus' and Muslims' protests against the state in different times have shown the possibility of ethnic conflict in Terai-Madhes. Pathak and Uprety (2009) argue that this struggle between the indigenous nationalities and the immigrants from India is fuelling the growth of ethnic militancy. Further, imposing a single identity as Madhesi violates the ILO Convention No. 169[18] and rights of indigenous nationalities. Nevertheless, it also escalates social imbalance among different caste and ethinic groups.

In the context of languages spoken in Madhes, Madhesi politicians, activists and scholars, referring to the census of 2001, argue that there are 22 different Madhesi languages[19] (Yadav 2007). Census has categorised all the languages used in this region as languages of Terai the status of which is shown in Table 1. But some scholars have interpreted all the languages used in the region as Madhesi languages. Disagreeing with them, Urdu speaking Muslims and Tharu-speaking Tharus say that, even though they reside in Madhes, they are not Madhesi and their language is not Madhesi language. But Gupta (2010) and Jha (1993) deny the existence of separate Tharu language whereas Chaudhary (2007) counter-argues the former two.

Table 1 Major languages in Terai-Madhes

S.N.	*Major languages*	*Speakers*	*Percentage in total*
1	Maithali	2797582	12.30
2	Bhojpuri	1712536	7.53
3	Tharu	1331546	5.86
4	Awadhi	560744	2.47
5	Bajjika	237947	1.05
6	Urdu	174840	0.77
7	Rajbansi	129829	0.57
8	Hindi	105765	0.47
9	Santhali	40260	0.18
10	Jhangar	28615	0.13
11	Bangla	23602	0.10
12	Marwari	22637	0.10
13	Angika	15892	0.07
14	Dhimal	17308	0.074
15	Khariya	1575	0.006
16	Kisan	489	0.002
17	Koche	54	0.0002
18	Meche	3301	0.01
19	Nepalese symbolic languages*	5743	0.03

Source: CBS (2003)

* It covers not merely the Madhesi people but Nepali population as a whole using Nepali symbolic language.

Similarly, Pahadi people residing in Madhes have their languages and cultures different from those of the Madhesis (Gurung 2001).

The word 'Pahadi' is locally used for all the hill-origin people living in Terai-Madhes. They may be the ethnic or the non-ethnic people from the hill (Pradhan and Shrestha 2005). The language of each hill ethnic groups, including Nepali, is considered as Pahadi language in Madhes (Gaige 2009). This also shows the variety of languages in Madhes.

At present, non-Madhesi group covers indigenous people, Muslims and hill-origin people living in Terai-Madhes (Gellener 2007). In local understanding, 'Madhesi' refers to those people living in Terai-Madhes; whose lifestyle, food habits, dress, language and culture are alike with the people of Uttar Pradesh and Bihar states of India (Gaige 2009; Gellner 1997 and Yadav 2006b). Some Madhesi people and Madhesi elite politicians prefer to call the people of hill-origin as 'Nepali' or 'Pahadi' and themselves as 'Madhesi'.[20] But after the uprising in Terai-Madhes in 2007, this preference is little bit changed. Politically conscious Madhesis now prefer to be called first as Madhesis, then as Nepalis. On the other hand, the hill-origin people living in Madhes are found claiming themselves as Nepali-speaking Madhesis. They argue the all people living in Madhes are Madhesi; only languages and cultures are different. But this argument is discarded by the government's provision of reservation to Madhesi on the basis of which hill-origin people residing in Madhes can not apply for reservation. It seems that this identity dilemma is day by day fuelling the conflict in Terai-Madhes as the tug of war between the groups does not seem to end easily.

1.3 Demography

Terai-Madhes covers 34,019 square kilometre land which is 23.1 per cent of the country's total land area (147,181 square kilometres) (CBS 2009). According recent preliminary report of Central Bureau of Statistics (CBS) Census of 2011, the southern plain region holds 50.15 per cent of the national population with density 392.[21] Some scholars have divided Terai-Madhes demography into two-fold. The first is Madhesi group. It refers to the historically, politically and socially marginalised and discriminated people. The next is Teraivasi (dwellers of Terai) which covers all the ethnic and caste groups living in this region (Yadav 1997 as cited in Bhattachan 2008). However, for the purpose of the book, which deals on the present context of conflict, we have categorised the population of Terai-Madhes into Madhesi and Non-Madhesi groups.

The data on Madhesi population is controversial due to the lack of clear provision in census. According to the census of 2001, Madhes covers 48.4 per cent of the total population (CBS 2001). Madhesi politicians and activists still claim that Madhes consists more than 51 per cent of the country's population (Yadav 2007) whereas some other studies claim that there are only 41 per cent Madhesis in total population (Yadav 2006a, 2006b). The preliminary report of Central Bureau of Statistics (CBS), the southern plain region holds 50.15% of the national population.[22] It automatically clarifies that Madhesi population is below than 50.15% because there are also hill-origin people included in significant number among them. This data should be looked in the context that Shah (2006) has stated that the hill-origin people consisted 36 per cent of Terai-Madhes population in the census of 2001. Disgruntling, Gupta (2006) argues this as a conspiracy to downsize the number of Madhesis. Furthermore, Pathak and Uprety (2009) argue that large number of Indian migrants have acquired citizenship certificate that increased the population of Terai-Madhes. Madhesi activists claim Madhesi people cover 41-51 per cent or more than that of national population. But they seem biased while claiming the number of total population. It seems that while referring to the population in Terai-Madhes, they show large number including the people from hill-origin who are residing there. By doing so, it becomes easier for them to claim that over 50 per cent of population reside in Terai-Madhes. But while sharing the benefits and other privileges, the Madhes leaders tend to exclude the hill-origin people. This has been considered as an opportunist approach backed by an unscientific claim and ultimately a source of new form of discrimination and communal conflict.

Amidst this hot debate, Gurung (2005) had written that Pahadis constitute 66.2%, Madhesis does so 28.4 per cent, and others (including religious groups such as Muslims and Sikhs) 5.4 per cent of the total population in Nepal. This percentage for Madhesi population is quite near to Shah (2006) who writes it as being 31 per cent. Hence, actual number, definition and categorisation of the Madhesi people are in controversy, heavily politicised and selectively interpreted. Including Tharus and Muslims, Madhesi population covers 31.34 per cent of the total population of the state. But, when Tharus and Muslims completely deny to be known as Madhesis, the state categorised them as Terai people. Hence, if we deduct the population of Muslims and Tharus from the Madhesi population, the latter goes down to 20.52 per cent. Still there are other ethnic and indigenous groups[23] who seek different identity than being Madhesi showing the possibility of the further decrease in the claimed number of Madhesi population. Table 2 elaborate the available data on the population distribution in Terai-Madhes.

Table 2 Population in Terai-Madhes (Except the hill-origin people)

S. N.	*Terai caste and ethnic groups*	*Total*	*Percentage of total Terai population*
1.	Tharus	1533879	21.13
2.	Muslims	971056	13.38
3.	Yadav	895423	12.33
4.	Teli	304536	4.19
5.	Chamar/Harijan/Ram	269661	3.71
6.	Koiri	251274	3.46
7.	Kurmi	212842	2.93
8.	Dhanuk	188150	2.59
9.	Musahar	172434	2.37
10.	Dusad/Paswan/Pasi	158526	2.18
11.	Sonar	145088	1.99
12.	Kewat	136953	1.88
13.	Brahmin	134496	1.85

14.	Baniya	126,971	1.74
15.	Mallah	115986	1.60
16.	Kalwar	115606	1.59
17.	Hajam/Thakur	98169	1.35
18.	Kanu	95826	1.32
19.	Rajbanshi	95812	1.32
20.	Sudi	89846	1.24
21.	Lohar	82637	1.14
22.	Tatma	76512	1.05
23.	Khatwe	74972	1.03
24.	Dhobi	73413	1.01
25.	Nuniya	66873	0.92
26.	Kumhar	54413	0.74
27.	Danuhar	53229	0.73
28.	Haluwai	50583	0.69
29.	Rajput	48454	0.66
30.	Kayastha	46071	0.63
31.	Badhae	45975	0.63
32.	Marwari	43971	0.60
33.	Santhal/Satar	42698	0.58
34.	Jhangar/Dhagar	41764	0.57
35.	Bantar	35839	0.49
36.	Barae	35434	0.48
37.	Kahar	34531	0.47
38.	Gangai	31318	0.43
39.	Lodha	24738	0.34
40.	Rajbhar	24263	0.33
41.	Dhimal	19537	0.26
42.	Bing/Binda	18720	0.25
43.	Bhediyar/Gaderi	17729	0.24
44.	Nurang	17522	0.24
45.	Tajpuriya	13215	0.18
46.	Chidimar	12296	0.16

47.	Mali	11390	0.15
48.	Bengali	9860	0.13
49.	Dom	8931	0.12
50.	Kamar	8761	0.12
51.	Meche	3763	0.05
52.	Halkhor	3621	0.04
53.	Punjabi	3054	0.04
54.	Kisan	2876	0.03
55.	Koche	1429	0.02
56.	Dhuniya	1231	0.02
57.	Jaine	1015	0.01
58.	Munda	660	0.00
59.	Kuswadiya/Patharkata	552	0.00
	Total	**7,256,384**	**100**

Source: CBS (2003)

End note

1. Geographically, the southern plain region of Nepal bordering with India is known as the Terai-Madhes region. Yet, the political debate on whether to call this region 'Terai' or 'Madhes' is still going on, the government, after series of discussions with the concerned stakeholders, termed the region as 'Terai-Madhes' in the Interim Constitution-2007. So, we also have used the term 'Terai-Madhes' throughout this book to refer to this region and also to avoid any controversies over this semantic debate. However, the terms 'Madhes' and 'Terai' may have been interchangeably used somewhere referring to the place in the southern plain land of Nepal.
2. The CPN (M) and the Unity Centre united in January 2009 and the name CPN (M) was changed into the United Communist Party of Nepal (Maoist) or UCPN (M). Small breakaway faction of the CPN (M) kept its original name CPN (M) even after the formation of the UCPN (M). Hence, UCPN (M) is used throughout this book to avoid the confusion with the name of the breakaway faction.
3. At present, Ganga Holy river of Hindus lies in Uttarakhand in India.
4. At present, Yamuna River lies in Uttarakhand in India.
5. At present, Ambala is a district which lies in the Haryana state of India.
6. At present, Prayag lies on Uttar Pradesh of India.

7. Interview taken with advocate Satya Mohan Joshi (Tharu) in Kathmandu on 9 December 2009
8. For details, see http://www.gorkhapatra.org.np/detail.gopa.php?article_id=15741&cat_id=4 retrieved on 13th October 2011.
9. For details, see http://www.gorkhapatra.org.np/detail.gopa.php?article_id=15741&cat_id=4 retrieved on 13th October 2011.
10. C. K. Lal (1998) 'Non-resident Indians in Nepal' *The Kathmandu Post*, 29 November 1998.
11. For details, see interview with Sadrul Miya Haque, independent Constituent Assembly (CA) member in *Nepali Times* of 5 February 2010.
12. Some caste groups listed as Madhesi are Bote, Danuwar, Darai, Kumal, Majhi, Raji, Tharu, Baniya, Bhumihar, Brahmin, Badhai, Sutihar, Chamar, Harijan, Dhobi, Batar, Dushadh, Paswan, Halawai, Dom, Kanu, Mehettar, Tatma, Ganajain, Kayastha, Barai, Bin, Chidimar, Kahar, Dhuniya, Kamar, Lodh, Kewat, Kawarath, Khatri, Kumhar, Mali, Kurmi, Shikari, Kushwaha, Rauniyar, Malah, Nishad, Rastogi, Mushahar and Kathbaniya among others.
13. For details, see "Govt lists 92 caste groups as Madhesi", *Republica National Daily* of 27 February 2009.
14. Based on a focus group discussion with Madhesi Dalits by Suman Babu Paudel in Janakpur on 21 February 2010
15. For detail, see http://www.thaIndian.com/newsportal/world-news/Nepal-muslims-give-ultimatum-to-maoist-government_100164875.html accessed on 31 July 2010.
16. Right to Self Determination is very regularly used in Nepal with diverse interpretation. Literatures and individual interpretation often misinterpret it as a Right to Secession and very few writings have provided genuine interpretation of ILO 169.
17. Phone interview with Advocate Satya Mohan Joshi (Tharu) on 14 August 2011
18. Convention No.169 is a legally binding international instrument open to ratification, which deals specifically with the rights of indigenous and tribal peoples. Today, it has been ratified by 20 countries. Once it ratifies the Convention, a country has one year to align legislation, policies and programmes to the Convention before it becomes legally binding. Countries that have ratified the Convention are subject to supervision with regards to its implementation (ILO Website).
19. Categorised as Maithili, Bhojpuri, Tharu, Urdu, Awadhi, Bajjika, Rajbamshi, Ghangad, Marwadi, Santhali, Angika, Panjabi, Bangala,

Dhimal, Meche, Uria, Hariyanwi, Asaamese, Kisan, Sindhi, Mangai and Hindi.

20. Based on the field visit carried out by Śuman Babu Paudel in Mahottari, Janakpur and Saptari on different dates in 2010
21. For details, see Preliminary Report of the Census-2011 by CBS.
22. For details, see Preliminary Report of the Census-2011 by CBS.
23. There are some very small groups such as Meche, Kishan, Satar, Jhangad, Tajpuria etc. The Central Bureau of Statistics has grouped them as 'The other Terai groups'.

2

Historical Exclusion and Structural Discrimination

2.1 Context of exclusion and discrimination

It is a universal principle for the state to provide equal attention to its all people. On one hand, the Terai-Madhes of Nepal did not get adequate attention from the state since long years (Yadav 2006a; Pathak and Uprety 2009) in comparison to the capital Kathmandu and other cities. On the other, opportunistic behaviour and elite nature of Terai-Madhes leadership and their vested interest to control power and resources at the cost of poor, marginalised and excluded people kept this region disadvantaged. Despite all these weaknesses, there are more infrastructures, productivity and economic scopes in Terai-Madhes than those are in hill and mountainous region. But the representation in the state apparatus in the past was mainly dominated by certain elite group making marginalised people unable to participate in the state-level decision-making (UNDP 2004). However, this region is far better than far-west and mid-west hill regions of Nepal in terms of economy, opportunities and representation (ibid). Geographical discrimination was, of course, a common political character in Nepal until 1990. Terai-Madhes is more advantageous in this respect compared to the hinterlands in hills and mountains. A bird's eye view over such matters shows that marginalisation, exclusion and discrimination in Terai-Madhes go beyond geography and reaches caste, class and gender dimension. Vertical exploitation, capture of resources (e.g. land) and power by few elites is more than serious in Terai-Madhes. The socio-economic analysis of the structure of marginalisation, exclusion and discrimination depicts that they are more the issues of elite versus non-elite and powerful versus powerless people.

Hangen (2010) claims that geographic discriminations in Nepal had begun after the unification of the modern Nepal under the leadership of Prithvi Narayan Shah[1]. Shah is presumed to have imposed uniform culture and language (of Nepali hill people) in the name of national integrity. Such impositions restricted the linguistic and cultural freedom of other ethnic groups. Gaige (2009) argues that this imposition benefited Khas people[2] in most of the opportunities. However, this argument is too superficial, general and insufficient to internalise the highly skewed power relation in Terai-Madhes. It was not the Khas people who always benefited but the powerful elites in Terai-Madhes had more widely exploited the opportunities in the southern region. It is evident from the fact that Terai-Madhesi upper castes are the most advanced Nepalis in terms of recent indices on human development.

Since the establishment of modern Nepal, the state had been building single national identity by assimilating all ethnicities through language and culture. This way the ruling elites not only controlled territories but also imposed their single culture on the other social, cultural and religious groups. Discrimination stretched over the country affecting many communities in hills and mountains generally and Terai-Madhes specifically (ICG 2007). The Civil Code (Muluki Ain) promulgated in 1854 by the autocratic Rana Prime Minister Jung Bahadur Rana (Kunwar) also enhanced these kinds of domination and caste-based discrimination (Pradhan and Shrestha 2005). The policies and Acts promulgated that time prioritised the cultures of upper castes and Khas hill people. They authenticated systematic discrimination strictly against the non-Khas groups making these groups underrepresented in state affairs

(ICG 2007). Fuelling the woe, raising voice against these biasness or discrimination was unimaginable till 1991 because of the frequent undemocratic rules (Middleton and Schneiderman 2008). However, the situation witnessed a rapid change after the political change of 1990.

Whatever the history was, one must admit that there are two extremes observed in the advocacy and literatures on exclusion and discrimination in Nepal. First, attempts have been made to re-examine the activities of the past from the indicator of the present, which is neither logical nor scientific. Hence, it is generating a lot of problems. Second, the historical, demographic and bio-physical realities are interpreted as per the conveniences. For example, while making political bargaining for the creation of more electoral constituencies during the election to the Constituent Assembly (CA), hill-origin people residing in Terai-Madhes were counted to demonstrate large population whereas the same population were not included when the opportunities came to harvest the benefits such as reservation quotas. Another instance is the selective denial of reality. The hill-origin people who are residing in Terai-Madhes for, generations are not recognised as Terai-Madhesis. But contradictorily, a recent migrant taking Nepalese citizenship or a woman from an adjoining state of India residing in Nepal after marrying a Nepali man can be a Madhesi. This sort of contradiction and duality is always manipulated as per the conveniences of the people of vested interest by the Madhesi leaders.

The reestablishment of multiparty democracy in 1990 provided space for 'suppressed' voices (Gellener 2007). Every ethnic and marginalised groups got equal rights and opportunities legally. However, the Constitution of Nepal 1990 also gave inclination to a particular religion (Hinduism) and language (Nepali). Although the diverse groups are considered equal by the law, all the constitutional provisions were not effectively implemented. Even after the promulgation of this Constitution, the Election Commission had denied to register the parties with ethnic agenda till 1991 (Gellner 2005).

Hangen (2007) criticises that in democratic system, many ethnic and marginalised groups were taken under consideration by governments, but Madhesi were not. Multiparty democracy and different governments in this system took several initiatives to end the discrimination and bring equality. Changes in laws and policies and establishment of different commissions were some examples. However, discrimination and exclusion had roots in every society. The discrimination, exclusion and marginalisation nurtured by few Madeshi elite groups were much stronger in Terai-Madhes compared to those in hills and mountains. This ethnic and caste issues took long time to dismantle this structural bottleneck throughout the country. The state started reservation system in 2002. There was space for women, Dalit and ethnic people (Whelpton et al. 2008); but was not for the Madhesis even though they were marginalised like the others (Hangen 2007).

The discrimination and exclusion within Madhesi community is high, as only few Madhesi elites are capturing power and resources. The people in southern plain have deep cultural relationship with the bordering states of India. Their complexion and languages also resembles with those of Indians. Burkert (1997) claims that they have been strongly influenced by Indian political actors only because of this physical and cultural feature. But the Madhesi people claim that they have been treated as quasi-foreigners (Gaige 2009) or as second class citizens (Yadav 2007) by the state even in their own homeland. This sentimental perception is deliberately and systematically used by Madhesi-elites to sustain their power and influence. Till 1950, they had to obtain entry permit to be in Kathmandu valley (Yadav 2006b and Yadav 2007). Madhesi people complain that the state has always suspected over the Nepalese patriotism in them. Referring to the historical incidents, Pathak and Uprety (2009) write that in Anglo-Gurkha war (1814-1816 AD), Madhes dwellers were closer with the British East India Company. Large number of Madhesis voluntarily fought against Gurkha during that war. The Madhesi were alleged to be the follower of British and adversary of Nepalis.

Even it is said people of the Terai regions were uncooperative with Gurkhali (ibid.). Since that time, loyalty of Madhesi people became matter of suspicion for Nepal that caused Madhesis to be continually marginalised and discriminated from the state affairs.

After the re-introduction of democracy in 1990, governments formed different commissions in different times to end the discrimination. But no safe space was created for the Madhesi people (Gellener 2007). Then His Majesty's Government introduced a roadmap on recruitment in civil services for a period of five years from April 2004. It proposed reservation 20 per cent for women, 10 per cent for Dalits and 10 per cent for ethnic people. But still there was no reservation for the Madhesis (Yadav 2006b). However, one should not be tempted by a possibly misleading interpretation that no Madhesis got reservation in this phase as women, Dalits and ethnic people were also residing in Terai-Madhes who were eligible to get the reservation under this provision.

Concerning the discrimination of Madhes and Madhesis, Lal (2002: 101) writes, "...for the Kathmandu elite, this flat piece of territory has historically been an area that needs to be exploited; its resources are useful, but its people are a liability". But this argument also seems insufficient because the Terai-Madhesi leaders are always blaming the state but keeping quite themselves on the exploitation over the poor and marginalised people within the region. Sukhdev Shah[3] a Madhesi scholar goes beyond blaming the state and the hill people for the deplorable condition of Madhes. Though Madhesi leaders advocate for inclusion of Madhesi and their rights, they every time forgot Madhes after getting political position and power. Rather these Madhesi parties divided themselves between camps and gangs depending on who promised them the largest attractions for personal gain. This tendency was frequently observed mainly during the share of cabinet posts and practice of nepotism in political appointments.[4]

Shah (2006) sharply criticises that the discrimination is so high that Madhesi people have almost lost the sense of belongingness to this nation. They are unsatisfied with the state's response to their needs. They have been claiming to have become the victim of the structural discrimination from the state. Yadav (2007) and Gupta (2010) have enlisted some of the issues over which Madhesi people are dissatisfied; they are following:

1. Resettlement plan and over migration
2. Under-representation in electoral process
3. Citizenship issue
4. Language and custom rights
5. Under-representation in state apparatus, and
6. Economic distribution and development disparity

Besides, placement of the east-west highway, land reform, ban to establish factories near border, naming of towns after the name of kings and royal members, policies that deforested the region, 'biased' integrated development projects, 'unfair' census are also listed as the issues of dissatisfaction. But the following paragraphs discuss only the select six issues considered the prominent ones in today's Madhes debate.

2.2 Resettlement plan and over migration

The Panchayat government[5] had introduced resettlement plan in Terai-Madhes in the mid 1980s. This region was a convenient place to immigrate after the eradication of Malaria. The government facilitated retired armies and Nepali speakers to settle here. Gupta (2010) argues that this had been conspiringly designed to make Madhesi people fall under minority. This process is also termed by some writers as 'Nepalisation' or 'Pahadisation' of Madhes (Yadav 2006a). The counter-argument says that this process of the settlement of retired Indian and British army of Nepali origin in border regions could have worked as a paramilitary force to prevent smuggling and raid by Indian bandit gangs (Gaige 2009). The focus group discussion by the authors in Janakpur and Rajbiraj have also found some people as much displeased as Gupta (2010) and

Yadav (2007) are on the resettlement plan and over migration in Madhes.[6] People were frequently complaining for they have been behaved as 'conquered people' or 'illegal Indian migrants'.[7]

The enhanced economic opportunities, abundant land, forest resources and resettlement programme launched by the state encouraged people's flow from Nepalese hills and neighbouring India into Madhes in 1960s and 1970s. Large area of forest was cleared for farming and settlement in different parts of Madhes. The gradual influx of hill people along the flat region limited Terai-Madhesis in the southern border (Yadav 2007). Yadav (2006b) alleges that the resettlement plan was the strategy of Pahadi politicians, especially King Mahendra, to weaken Terai-Madhesis from their own land by creating social, political and cultural pressure (Yadav 2007). Defying this allegation, Adhikari et al. (2006) argue that this kind of resettlement plan was a need to manage haphazard migration of hill people in Terai-Madhes after the Malaria eradication program.

Economically developed Terai-Madhes area attracts huge immigration for economic opportunities. Further, controlling migration process is impractical in a globalised context as opportunities determine the degree and intensity of migration. Table 3 shows the population shift that describes inflow of the hill people into Terai-Madhes.

Table 3 Population change in Terai-Madhes

Year	*Pahadi population*	*Madhesi population*	*Total*	*Percentage of hill people*	*Percentage of Madhesi population*
1952	142,000	2,246,000	2,388,000	5.9	94.1
1981	2,795,000	3,762,000	6,557,000	42.6	57.4
1991	3,444,000	5,262,000	8,706,000	39.6	60.4
2001	4,120,000	7,092,000	11,212,000	36.7	63.3

Source: Shah (2006)

Some advocacy studies have used this data on change of the population to show anger over the heavy migration of hill people into Terai-Madhes. But, few scholars have analysed demographic data minutely. Most of the scholars have pointed migration as the cause of the sudden rise of hill population in Madhes especially in 1981. But the reason of the decrease of such a percentage after 1981 should also be analysed. Hachhethu (2007) has tried to explore its answer to some extent. He argues that in the past, Nepal was divided into 32 districts. There were only nine Terai and three inner Terai districts thereby constituting limited numbers of Madhesi population. But when the government divided the country into 75 districts in 1963, Terai covered 20 districts. This region included the large areas of Shiwalik Range[8] and mid-hills. This caused some hill regions to fall under Terai. It constituted the population in Terai to be higher including the Shiwalik Range and mid-hill dwellers.

On total land area of Terai-Madhes, mid-hill and Shiwalik cover 11,041 square kilometres and the flat plain including inner Madhes covers 23,068 square kilometres which are respectively 34.2 and 65.8 per cent of total Terai-Madhes (Shah 2006). Due to this distribution in 1963, obviously the large number of hill population had to be counted under the Terai population. Thus, the high percentage of hill people is seen in this region during 1981 census. The hill people population has not increased since 1981. If there were continuous migration, the hill people percentage should have increased even after 1981. Hence, it is not only migration and resettlement plan, but also the re-demarcation of the boundaries (Shah 2008) that generated the fluctuation of the data on the migration of hill people in Terai-Madhes. The number of Madhesi people in Kathmandu valley and other hill towns has also increased over time. Hence, it is a natural migration process and therefore does not justify the claim of some writers and regional leaders.

Even though the resettlement and migration is seen as the 'conspiracy' to rule over Terai-Madhes by the hill-elite, in the different light, Gaige (2009) argues that these programmes were need-based. There was a heavy flow of people from western Nepal to eastward and even to the different districts of India and Bhutan. He says that the resettlement programmes were launched to stop Nepalis' migration to India. Estimated food grain production declined by 11.3 per cent in the mountain and 5.7 per cent in the hills due to land degradation, soil erosion and less productivity during 1970/71-1980/81. Hill area was suffering from food scarcity and lack of land due to increased population (Gurung 1989; Adhikari et al. 2006). Large number of Nepali hill population started migrating to India along the hill from west to east. Referring to the Indian census of 1961, Gaige (2009) has stated that Nepali speakers in the districts of west Bengal, Sikkim and Assam increased significantly within 60 years. The number people speaking the languages of Nepalese origin increased by 64.4 percent in India during 1891 and 1921 most of whom were deposited in Bengal and Sikkim (Davis 1968 as cited in Gurung 1989). During the same period, a large number of hill people migrated to Bhutan, Burma and some other countries too. Fearing the heavy migration of Nepalis to India, the resettlement programme had been launched. But after the Malaria eradication programme, hill people spontaneously started to migrate to the plain region.

Chaudhary (2007) and Gurung (1989) also write that till 1950s, Nepalis used to migrate to the eastern Indian states and Burma. But after the Terai-Madhes was declared safe to reside, it became a new destination for the hill people. The volume of spontaneous migration to the lowland was much higher than that during the resettlement programme (ibid). No matter whatever the blame is there on resettlement programme, one must also take into account that the Ranas had also tried to encourage the migration of hill people by bringing a forest policy. Referring to Landon (1928: 252), Adhikari et al. (2006) writes that the aim of the policy was to cut the trees in massive to generate the money by selling timbers and taxing the expanded fertile land. But at that time, the policy was taken as a wise plan which could decrease the heavy outflow of Nepali population to Indian districts by extension of fertile lands in the southern plain.

Citizens have natural rights to migrate from one place of the state to another without any obligations. Disregarding this natural law, many Madhesi leaders are claiming that the hill people have displaced them from their land and made them minorities in their own land. It is interesting to notice that most of the areas where hill migration is found high are either the unused lands or the land occupied by not Madhesis but the Terai indigenous people (Hachhethu 2007; Gurung 1989). Migration of the hill people to Terai-Madhes has become a matter of grief. It is termed as a planned 'Nepalisation' of Terai-Madhes.

The allegation remains silent on the Indian immigrants who got assimilated as Nepali Madhesis. According to 1950's treaty between Nepal and India, Indian people can participate in industrial and economic activity in Nepal. They can come here and reside easily; but they do not have the legal status of being Nepali citizens. Many recent Indian immigrants have taken citizenship certificate and are getting privilege of being Madhesis. Hence, if the logic that the immigration in Terai-Madhes has narrowed Madhesi people's opportunities over limited resources and opportunities is valid, the immigration of Indian people is equally responsible as is that of the Nepalese hill people. But the leaders, analysts and activists blaming hill people for all the problems of Madhes do not discuss about this sort of immigration which had started before the immigration of the Nepalese hill people.

Gaige (2009) states that the hill migrants were more conspicuous than the Indian migrants to recognise. It was because the formers had noticeable difference in their physique, complexion and languages, but the latter did not have so because of the similarities in physique, complexion and languages with the Madhesis. Indeed, the Indian migrants started coming into Nepal already before Malaria eradication (Adhikari et al. 2006). From the very beginning of the Rana Regime, governments had been encouraging the migration of the hill people into Terai-Madhes.

But they were not so fruitful not only because of unfamiliar environment, but also because of the fear of Malaria. Gaige (2009), Upreti (2006) and Majumdar (2006) argue that in such a situation, governments let the flow of Indian migrants to develop the economy of Terai-Madhes. Like government resettlement programme for hill people, Rana governments had also facilitated the Indian migrants by providing essential accessories for housing and others (Regmi 1978 and Adhikari et al. 2006). Further, in order to develop the newly acquired territories known as Naya Muluk[9] (New Territory) and other Terai-Madhes districts and also to appropriate income for his family members and relatives, Prime Minister Jung Bahadur Rana introduced a new provision in the first Civil Code of Nepal in 1862. It had stated that the foreigners residing in Nepal could purchase and sell lands in Nepal. This led large-scale migration of Indian businessmen and entrepreneur to purchase land in Nepal, which was followed by migration of the tillers as well (Kansakar 2003). This resulted into the large scale immigration of people from Indian cities into the Terai. In the eastern Terai, the Yadav community harvested this opportunity, which can be seen in their considerable presence there. Some of them had even settled in these places before that (Kansakar 2001). The open border and availability of large chunk of land and increasing development in the Terai regions contiguous to India had further encouraged immigration across the southern border. It is also due to the lower density of population in Terai compared to adjoining Indian districts (Gurung 1989).

In fact, the inflow of Indian people to Terai-Madhes is seemingly higher than the migration of hill people in the region. Gaige (2009) again argues that the migration rate of the hill people into Terai-Madhes was lower than that of Indian origin plain people there. He points that, among the migrants, 59 per cent were Indian plain people, 35 per cent were hill people and six percent were tribal indigenous. He further describes that Nepalisation has not made any kind of effect on Madhesi majority settlement areas; settlement of hill people on those areas were low except in some urban city areas. Rather, majority of hill people found settling on ethnic and tribal people's areas. So, Madhesi people themselves are consolidating and extending their power and control on their places. Madhesi majority places have not been altered by the resettlement and migration because of the less number of hill migrants. Gaige puts evidences that Nepalisation has mainly taken place on the far-eastern and far-western part of the country because they had high percentage of net migration compared to its total population and decennial increase (Gurung 1989).

2.3 Under-representation in electoral process

Under-representation due to the provisions in electoral process has been a nuisance for Terai-Madhes since years back. There was under-representation in electoral process of Madhesi in three ways: district re-demarcation, allocation of the electoral constituencies and distribution of them.

The district re-demarcation in 1963 is considered unjust. It is said that ignoring the ecological and social foundation, the demarcation has included varying portions of Shiwalik and mid-hills (Shah 2006). It is supposed to have increased the dominance of hill people in Terai-Madhes. This is also considered a point from where hill population, culture, practices and languages spread in the plains. This reduced the role of plain people in politics and decision-making.

The Constitution of 1990 was also not fully followed during the allocation of the electoral constituencies. This constitution had required increment of parliamentary constituencies as per the population increment. The population in Terai-Madhes increased from 43 per cent in 1991 to 48 per cent in 2001. But there was no increase in the number of constituencies (Hachhethu 2007). The mountain and the hill districts with even lower population had significant constituencies than the districts from Terai-Madhes had. As a result, there was larger representation from hills and mountains in both Houses. In the election to the parliament held in 1999, only 88 among 205 constituencies were from Terai-Madhes (Yadav 2007, EC 1999). Resultantly, there was less influence of plain people in national plans and policies. This became one of the scenes of tension and conflict.

There is also a debate on the way that constituencies in Nepal are distributed in a north-south strip pattern. By doing so, there would be sizeable hill portion in every constituency in Terai-Madhes. Hence, it has been claimed that the constituencies have been systemised to weaken the influence of Terai-Madhes (ICG 2007).

There were 88 electoral constituencies from 20 Madhes districts in 1999's parliamentary election. It was 42.92 per cent of total 205 constituencies in the country. But at present, the scenario has changed. People in Terai-Madhes demanded the number of constituencies there to be increased as there was increment in the number of constituencies in CA election. The third amendment in the Interim Constitution-2007 has addressed this issue to some extent. It made 20 Terai-Madhes districts contain 116 out of 240 constituencies for the First-Past-the-Post election system.[10] With this effect, this southern region covering 48.44 per cent of total population (CBS 2001) now hold 48.33 per cent of total constituencies.

Table 4 Change in number of constituencies in 20 Madhes districts

S.N.	*Districts*	*Number of constituencies*	
		Parliamentary election-1999	*CA election 2008*
1	Jhapa	6	7
2	Morang	7	9
3	Saptari	5	6
4	Siraha	5	6
5	Sunsari	5	6
6.	Sarlahi	5	6
7	Mahottari	4	6
8	Dhanusha	5	7

9	Bara	4	6
10	Parsa	4	5
11	Rupandehi	5	7
12	Kapilbastu	4	5
13	Chitwan	4	5
14	Dang	4	5
15	Banke	3	4
16	Bardiya	3	4
17	Kailali	4	6
18	Kanchanpur	3	4
19	Rautahat	4	6
20	Nawalparasi	4	6
	Total	**88**	**116**

Source: Adapted from Election Commission (1999 and 2008)

2.4 Citizenship issue

The major problems to the Madhesis are identity and citizenship. Citizenship certificate is a document that legally declares a person as a citizen of the state. So, it creates a legal relation between the state and individuals. Bauböck (2002) writes that in its complete sense, citizenship signifies membership in a self-governing community. By providing citizenship, the state facilitates citizens' accessibility to its resources. In Nepal, citizenship is a compulsory legal document even to get a job, create a bank account, compete in a public post and receive other state services. But in the past, many people from Terai-Madhes were bereft of the government services and other opportunities due to the lack of it.

It is alleged that the state doubted on the nationality of the people in Terai-Madhes and was cautious to issue citizenship to all people claiming citizenship. It might be mainly because of the resemblance of their physique, complexion and languages to those of the people in the bordering areas of India. Based on the criteria of citizenship defined by the Citizenship Act-1964 and the Constitution of 1990, the government scrutinised before issuing citizenship to those who did not have birth certificates and other documents to prove their Nepalese origin (Gupta 2010; Yadav 2006).

Some analysts and political activists claim that half of the people in Terai-Madhes were deprived of the basic legal documents. It may be either because they had come from India or the actual Nepalis did not prepare necessary documents required for citizenship. However, ignoring this reality, citizenship issue was blatantly politicised and sensationalised by the Madhesi parties instead of helping people to prepare required documents for citizenship for those who did not have. There is always politicisation and disagreement among different parties and the government on citizenship issues. Almost all of the Terai-Madhes-based parties made citizenship issue as their central slogan. Scholars are also divided regarding the strict nature of Citizenship Act-1964. Hachhethu (2007) claims that this Act was biased against the non-Nepali speakers as it intentionally complicated the process of getting citizenship. Upreti (2006) also admits it being a strict provision as it was brought during the autocratic Panchayat regime whereas Pathak and Uprety (2009) blames the Constitution of 1990 for additionally imposing a strict rule for the people to claim citizenship.

According to the Citizenship Act 1964 and the Constitution of 1990, general eligibilities to get Nepalese citizenship were:

(a) having birth certificate from Nepal,

(b) fluently speaking and writing Nepalese, and

(c) staying in Nepal for at least fifteen year (for citizenship by naturalisation) (Upreti 2006).

Some of the people in Terai-Madhes were not able to show their birth-certificate. Linguistically different, they did not have fluency in Nepali speaking and writing. Also, they did not have any legal document on their stay in Nepal for fifteen years. Upreti (2006) argues that getting citizenship around and before 1950 was much liberal than the situations after 1964 and 1990. During the 1950s, children having either of their father or mother as Nepali citizen, people married with a Nepali citizen or those living in Nepal permanently for at least five years were eligible to get citizenship certificate. Nepal's high dependency on India and its limited exposure with rest of the world was the reason behind that liberal law on citizenship (Gaige 1975 and Upreti 2006). But, to some extent, there was no need of strict laws before 1950s as there was limited inflow of migration of the Indian people. This is why Rana rulers were encouraging Indians to settle in Terai-Madhes before 1950s and they did so by also providing physical assistance. However, over time the immigration rules and getting citizenship certificate became strict globally.

The data on how many Madhesis have not got citizenship certificate is also ambiguous. Different political parties have different claim on numbers. Thus, this also has been a matter of grave politicisation. A number of commissions were formed on citizenship, but the problem is not solved yet. The citizenship commission formed by the government under the chairpersonship of Dhanapati Upadhyaya in 1994 reported that almost 3.5 million Nepalis did not have citizenship certificates (Neupane 2000). The Supreme Court had to intervene over this issue because of the high debate and politics. In 1997, then government distributed citizenship certificate to 34,900 Madhesis. It also passed the Citizenship Act in 1999. But the Supreme Court cancelled these issued citizenship certificates and declared the process 'unconstitutional' (Hachhethu 2007). The people in Terai-Madhes felt being the victims of injustice as again it was blatantly politicised. Instead of engaging in the root cause of such restricted legal provision, Madhesi politicians followed easy way to politicise it. Citizenship issue became a hot topic at the time of election for every government coming into power. All of the political parties came with attractive slogans; but the application did not accord the slogans. Sometimes, governments tried to distribute certificates to get public favour. But the number of Terai-Madhes people without citizenship certificate has not gone down significantly. Referring the Citizenship Act and the flooding number of people demanding it, the responsible authorities pointed large inflow of Indian immigrants, their settlement and issue of nationality as the reasons behind making citizenship law strict. But indeed, it badly impeded genuine Madhesi Nepali citizens (Upreti 2006; Mathema 2011).

Pathak and Uprety (2009) view that citizenship issue has become unending and complicated due to the Peace and Friendship Treaty signed in 1950 with India. Article 6 and 7 of the Treaty encouraged the migration of citizens of both countries. Article 6 states that "Nationals of the other, in its territory, national treatment with regard to participation in industrial and economic development of such territory", Article 7 mentions, "... on a reciprocal basis, to the national of one country in the territories of the other the same privileges on the matter of residence, ownership of property, participation in trade and commerce, movement and other privileges of similar nature" and affords the Nepalese nationals in Nepal protection from unrestricted competition". By such provisions, people from both countries do not need visa to visit one another's land. Many Nepalese went India and a large number of Indian-people came to Nepal and dissolved as Madhesis. It has been reported that most of Indian migrants now possess dual citizenship (KC 1998). They want to live a life as citizens of the both country, they are likely to settle wherever they get good opportunity and success.[11]

Expanding immigration of Indian people into Nepal is evidenced by the high concentration of Indians in Terai-Madhes. Concerning this, Gurung (1989) opines Indian migration into Nepal as a natural process. He reasons that when two adjoining areas with similar environment have differences in population density with no restrictions on mobility, the movement is obviously towards low density areas. Referring to Sen Gupta (1970), Gurung (1989) writes that mostly the flow was from Indian rural to Nepalese rural area. Comparatively, rural population pressure on land resources in Bihar and Uttar Pradesh, which are close to Nepal, was high. These regions had been taken as problematic regions based on high population density, growth rate, resource scarcity and low socio-economic development. They therefore had a high rate of out migration, almost more than 70% rural to rural. Due to the similarity of natural and cultural environment between the Terai-Madhes and the parts of these Indian states, it is reasonable to assume that sizeable proportion of migration was directed to Nepal.

The indication of migration from India is justified by the census reports of 1961, 1971, 1981, 1991 and 2001. The huge mass of India-born population documented in Nepal clarifies it (KC 1998). In 1961, among the foreign born population of Nepal, 96 per cent are of Indian birth and Terai only had 92.3 per cent of foreign born population. Among the foreign born population in only Terai region, 98.9 per cent were born in India. Census of 1971 has recorded 337,448 foreign born population in Nepal, among them 95.6 per cent were Indian born and 91.3 per cent of those resided in Terai districts. In census 1981, on total number of migrants in Terai, 94.3 per cent were born in India, 2.6 per cent in Bangladesh and 3.1 per cent in other countries. There were 94.4 per cent Indian-born migrants in eastern Nepal who were from Bihar. In western Nepal, there were 88.2 per cent migrants from Uttar Pradesh. In 1991, the foreign born population equalled 439,488 people, where 95.3 per cent were Indians. Over 80 per cent of foreign born population had obtained Nepali citizenship certificates (ibid.). Those foreign born settled in hill and mountain districts were the children of Nepalese in foreign militaries. Those people recorded as Burma-born, however, represent return migrants of Nepalese origin after the implementation of the Burmese Nationalisation Act in 1964. In 2001 census, Indian born population was 583,599 that is 95.97 per cent of 608,092 total foreign born population.

Table 5 Foreign born population in Nepal since 1961 to 2001

Country	1961	%	1971	%	1981	%	1991	%	2001	%
India	324159	96	322718	95.6	222278	95	418982	95.3	583599	95.97
China	8061	2.4	1534	0.5	2484	1.1			1295	0.21
Pakistan	2302	0.7					279	0.06		
Bangladesh							547	0.12	556	0.09
Bhutan							3159	0.72	2446	0.40
Sri Lanka and the Maldives							56	0.01		
Burma	1052	0.3	6364	1.9						
Malaya	1531	0.5								
Other Asian Countires	285	0.1	6131	1.8	7827	3.3	14523	3.3	17684	2.91
European countires			207	0.1			989	0.23	1497	0.25
Other countries			494	0.1			953	0.22	1015	0.17
Other/ Unstated	230	0.1			1453	0.6				
Total	**337620**	**100**	**337448**	**100**	**234039**	**100**	**439488**	**100**	**608092**	**100**

Source: Adapted from KC (1998) and Kansakar (2003)

Strict citizenship law can also be viewed as a legal provision that preserves the rights of its citizens by limiting the high competition with foreign born population for resources and opportunities in state. Concerning the effect of the immigration of foreign born population in Nepal, then His Majesty's Government in 1983 had formed a task-force led by Dr Harka Gurung to study the impact of internal and international migration in Nepal (Subedi 2007). It had suggested that the people from India were mostly skilled or semi-skilled workers that had caused displacement to local labourers or native workers. The study came out with recommendations on the management and regulation of the border. It prescribed the state to make provision of work permit for Indians and strict rules of citizenship to prevent local people's primary rights over resources and opportunities. It noted the illegal entry of Indian nationals into Nepal under the guise of local Madhesi people of the Terai. Subedi (2007) writes that the Gurung-led task-force was very much far-sighted. He re-emphasises that the unrestricted rules on entry and exit forever does not benefit both the countries. However, the report was not implemented. The Madhesi leaders were against the report and even against the border regulations. Certainly, open border has some advantages and disadvantages. KC (1998) argues that open border has helped both countries to develop harmonious socio-economic, cultural and religious relationship since a long run. To some extent, entrepreneurship and organisational skills of Indian side, their extensive contacts abroad and seasonal agricultural labourers in Terai-Madhes have all helped Nepalese economy rise. But he admits that continued immigration from India will create more pressure on available resources within country and will harm basic requirement in business and construction sectors in future. The study by Subedi (2007) has also seconded KC (1998) in this regard. As India is having nearly 1.5 billion people and if even small number of population from this enters Nepal because of the open border provision, it will cause huge demographic imbalance making it a serious matter of concern. Hence, seeking balance is important. A large number of Nepalis are also working in India as seasonal migrants entertaining the open border. Border control may cause immediate problems to their livelihoods (Subedi 2007). Hence, border regulation with certain provision is the balance between the two extremes given the complex nature of Indo-Nepal relation because of cultural, religious, economic and social inter-dependence.

Gurung (2010) has argued that there are two ways of protecting nationality from foreign immigration. It is either by keeping border tight or by making distribution of citizenship strict. This is not only the case in Nepal which had tightened the citizenship law to control over migration and save nationality. Gaige (2009) has given some example of the European states that made immigration laws strict. The large immigration from eastern and southern Europe to the US during the twentieth century led to restrictive US immigration legislation in 1924. Similar demands have recently received attention in the Great Britain because of the migration from South Asia and West Indies (ibid.).

The issue of strict citizenship law is not only the case of Nepal in South Asia. Upreti (2006) argues that most of South Asian countries have suffered from migration. It ultimately gave birth to conflicts among natives and migrants. So, the states are tightening the provisions on citizenship. He further exemplifies the case of migration and citizenship between India and Pakistan and argues that the states follow stricter rules in such cases during their hard times. Bangladesh, Bhutan and Sri Lanka are also facing similar problems and proceeded similarly (Nubin 2002 and Human Right Watch 2003).

Generally, the demand for restrictive citizenship regulation has arisen during the periods of large scale migration. Migration of Indians into Nepal is undoubtedly one of the factors that contributed to the restrictive citizenship regulations incorporated in 1962 (Gaige 2009, Upreti 2006). However, Citizenship Act of Nepal was amended in 2006 to make easy access to citizenship certificates. It privileged anyone born and permanently residing in Nepal since 1990 to be eligible for citizenship. The government distributed 1.5 million citizenship certificates in Terai-Madhes and 1.02 millions in the hills during January-April 2007.[12] There was a debate concerning the amendment. Some people even claimed that this amended Act will keep indigenous Terai people in minority in short period and could turn Nepal into Fiji.[13] The argument behind this claim is the massive inflow of Indian migrants because of the open border. However, this amendment has been taken as half-hearted because application for citizenship by birth was made valid for two years only until 26 November 2008 (Jha 2010). Although this amendment made large number of the people without citizenship eligible for it, Madhesi leaders are still dissatisfied with this initiative. They are arguing that the amendment in Citizenship Act has resolved some of the issues pertaining to identity; but still, there are some demands that this Act should be more liberalised to provide citizenship to the all the people of non-hill-origin residing in Terai-Madhes. Dissatisfied leaders still claim that the amendment in 2006 have only allowed citizenship to those born before 1990 but have not addressed the problems for those born after 1990.[14] However, this problem does not seem to be solved until and unless a scientific border regulation is agreed between Nepal and India. Citizenship for genuine Nepalis is still not a problem. Voters' electronic registration system in the Election Commission will also help in long run to solve this problem. However, Madhesi leaders are against this process. The hidden reason behind the objection is said to be the diminishing scope of manipulation of election by bringing people outside the electoral constitution.

It has been frequently reported that large number of Indian also got the citizenship certificate due to this amendment.[15] Further, this amendment made a large number of Bhutanese and other refugees eligible to get certificate as they were residing in Nepal since 1990. Jha (2010) notifies that 60 per cent of the over 100,000 Bhutani refugees living in Nepal have been granted Nepalese citizenship certificates due to this amendment. Similarly, the misuse of distribution of citizenship certificates, particularly to alleged criminals who are most wanted in India have been major concern regarding Nepal's security, peace and political representation even in future federations in Nepal (Pathak and Uprety 2009). Taking into account these all contexts, a question rises here, "Does the amendment and distribution process favour Madhesi people for the long-run?" Debates need to focus on these questions.

The state has full authority to protect its sovereignty and nationality. To keep it safe, the state can make any law and rule strict as required. But in the name of restriction, no state should keep its citizens away from their natural rights (Upreti 2006). When Nepalese Madhesis demand fair distribution of citizenship certificates with easy access to ensure their legal identity, the state must act responsibly. But when some vested interest group abuse citizenship issues as bargaining tool and means of fulfilling their political and individual interests, the state should take the issue seriously and respond firmly. Even some Madhesi politicians also accept this fact. They have said the distribution process was incorrect and demanded a probe to investigate on the citizenship distribution.[16] The careless distribution might cause them lose their identity and opportunities. If government distributed citizenship without proper investigation, large mass of Indian immigrants could access it which will obviously narrow down the opportunities of genuine Madhesi citizens. While interviewing with Madhesi students in Janakpur about liberalising Citizenship Act, most of the students were found saying that the state limited them by making the provision strict. The state kept them away from their basic rights; but later, by making the process liberal on the name of Madhesis, the state is again sharing Madhesi people's rights with the Indian immigrants. After getting citizenship certificate, they may join politics and may hold decision-making positions. So, if government is really serious about Madhesi issues and citizenship, the Citizenship Act should be amended in such a way that the true citizens of Nepal would be no more away from their right of possessing citizenship. If not, it may be the Pandora's Box in the future of peaceful, prosperous and just Nepal, especially because of Nepal's geo-political position surrounded by India in three sides.

2.5 Language and custom rights

Gellener (1997) opines that the state has allegedly imposed Khas language and culture in the name of national integration. So as to promote the Panchayati nationalism, the state, especially after 1950s, actively tried to influence the southern plain region economically, culturally and administratively (Hachhethu 2007 and Jha 1993). The national assimilation and acculturation moved forward by spreading Nepalese language and Khas culture (Hangen 2010).

Madhesis people had been demanding Hindi as the official language in Madhes since 1956. But the state ignored their cultural and linguistic rights (Yadav 2007). This imposition made large number of Madhesis difficult to get enrolled in the education system taught in non-Madhesi (Nepali) language. Pathak and Niraula

(2007) claim that the compulsion to use Nepalese language was also the reason for the lower empowerment of Madhesis. It ultimately fuelled conflict in the region. However, even though Hindi is not the mother-tongue of majority of Terai-Madhesi people, it is used by Madhesi elites as a powerful bargaining tool with government and softening tool with Indian establishment.

Language and nationalism became a hot debate when state declared Nepali language as the teaching language in government schools. Since then language issue became highly debated political issue in Madhes (Gaige 2009). Before 1956, Hindi was teaching language there (Gupta 2010). But National Education Planning Commission in 1956 recommended compulsion of Nepali language for both official and teaching purposes. Referring to a report from the same commission, Gaige (2009) writes that it justified the need of Nepalese language as the language in teaching with some arguments like:

- if the national language is made the medium of instruction, this would avoid preparing text books in many languages,
- it will be imperative to adopt a general policy to give status to a language which is spoken by the majority of the people,
- national language will be easier to learn than Hindi as no truly Hindi- speaking people inhabit in any part of the country,
- as an official language for a long time, Nepali language has been used everywhere and therefore is not difficult for the local people to understand,
- Nepali language bears a closer affinity with Hindi than any other local languages, and
- to solve the problems of multiplicity of language, stress and importance will have to be laid on one language, if the integrity and sovereignty of Nepal is to be maintained.[17]

As a result, Dr K. I. Singh's government banned teaching in Hindi language after 1957 (Gaige 2009). As the demand of Hindi was so popular in Madhes, the first elected Prime Minister

Bishweshor Prasad Koirala introduced this language in the curriculum in Madhes in 1959 (Nayak 2011). But it was revoked after the coup by King Mahendra. The King imposed a slogan *'Hamro Bhasa, Hamro Bhesh, Pran Bhanda Pyaro Chha'* (Our language and our costumes are dearer than our lives) (Gupta 2010). The constitution of 1959 declared 'Nepali in Devnagari script' as the national language. After this, the demand for Hindi and other languages became unlawful under the Panchayat tyranny.

After the restoration of democracy, hopes of marginalised groups awakened again. Discussions on rights remained no more an offence. The 1990's Constitution declared the rights to protect and promote one's own language and culture. But, it was not as good in practice as it was in words. Further, even after the Panchayat monopoly ended and multi-party system came into practice, the parliamentarians were unable to change their behaviour and practices. The Local Self-Governance Act of 1999 ensured that local bodies such as District Development Committees (DDCs), Village Development Committees (VDCs) and municipalities preserve and promote national languages. In the course of its implementation, Kathmandu Metropolitan City decided that Nepal Bhasa (Newari language) will be used as an additional official language and Rajbiraj Municipality and Dhanusha DDC decided that Maithili language will be used as an additional official language in their respective local bodies. But, in June 1999, the Supreme Court declared these all practices illegal. Non-Nepali speakers were disadvantaged as the Public Service Commission exams were held in the Nepalese language (Pradhan and Shrestha 2005; Bhattachan 2008). The naturalisation process also required fluency in Nepali in speaking and writing (Hachhethu 2007, Yadav 2006a and Yadav 2006b). It resulted into many non-Nepali speakers being deprived of citizenship certificates. Thus, the monolingual policy deprived the non-Nepali speakers such as Madhesis from many opportunities and services.

The politics of language and conflict has also created constitutional and political crisis. First Vice-President Paramanand

Jha, who hails from Madhes community, at the time of taking oath of his position and confidentiality, recited the texts in oath in Hindi language when he was required to take it in Nepalese language. Even after the Supreme Court ordered him to take oath in Nepali language, Jha refused. So, he lost his position for some times. It became an issue of huge political tension during the times when Nepal was preparing to conclude the peace process. More grave was the issue that Jha chose Hindi, not his own mother-tongue Maithili, language to take the oath. So, people suspected some Indian influence over the matter. The attraction of Madhesi leaders towards Hindi language instead of advocating further own mother-tongue made general people suspicious on their intention. Hence, many people stood against the behaviour of the Vice-President. The political parties realised the sensitivity of the case and later reached a negotiated settlement and amended the Interim Constitution that permitted people in government positions to take oath in their mother-tongue. Only after this amendment, Jha took oath in Maithali, not in Nepali and not even in Hindi. Arguments are there that say the Madhesi political leaders nowadays are prioritising Hindi than their own mother-tongue so as to appease India and secure own political future as India is still the kingmaker in Nepalese politics (Upreti 2009). And, it also does not seem false in the context of growing Indian influence in Madhes-based parties in Nepal. But the need of the hour is that such leaders should convince their people that they are indeed advocating for the genuine needs of the Madhesis, not their own. And, the state should also take into mind that all the languages and cultures should be equally given space for a democratic and prosperous future of overall Nepalis.

2.6 Under-representation in state apparatus

Terai-Madhesi People cover about 31 per cent of the total population, but they occupy fewer posts in judiciary, executive, legislature, constitutional bodies compared to their share in total population (Yadav 2007).

Table 6 shows the representation of different caste groups on gazetted level public service. It shows only Hill Brahmin community covers 70.06 per cent of gazetted level jobs. Following Brahmins, Chhetri covers 10.66 per cent, Newar covers 9.55 per cent, Janajatis (except Newar) holds 2.03 per cent and Madhesi group shares 6.69 per cent of gazetted level jobs. Among 52 special class officers of gazetted level, there are three from Madhesi and altogether 18 Madhesis in the first class out of 359 (5.01%) officers. In second class, there are 201 (10.2%) Madhesi among 1970 and 546 (6%) Madhesis in the third class gazetted employees. In total, there are 768 Madhesis in gazetted level. Although the Terai-Madhesi people hold around one third of the national population, their representation in government employment is poor but satisfactory than the Janjati and Dalit population. Still, the number of Madhesis in non-technical services is comparatively lower; but their representation in technical services is higher and satisfactory. They cover almost 34 per cent of total technical employees in the government (Biswakarma 2008). In the past 5-6 years, the situation is changed, however, due to promotions and new recruitments.

Table 6 Caste and ethnic composition in gazetted level employement

Caste/ethnic groups	*Special class*	*First class*	*Second class*	*Third class*	*Numbers*	*Percentage*
Brahmin	38 (73.3%)	217 (60.44%)	1140 (57.85%)	6643 (73.06)	8038	70.06
Chhetri	6 (11.5%)	51 (14.2%)	252 (12.8%)	915 (10%)	1224	10.66
Dalit	0	0	8 (0.4%)	22 (0.24%)	30	0.26
Newar	4 (7.7%)	63 (17.54%)	304 (15.45%)	725 (8%)	1096	9.55
Janajatis (excluding Newar)	0	7 (1.94%)	57 (2.9%)	175 (2%)	239	2.038

Madhesi, Muslim and Marwari	3 (5.7%)	18 (5.01%)	201 (10.2%)	546 (6%)	768	6.69
Other	1 (1.8%)	3 (0.84%)	8 (0.4%)	65 (0.7%)	77	0.67
Total	52	359	1970	9091	11,472	100
Percentage	**0.5**	**4.9**	**26.4**	**68.2**	**100**	**100**

Source: Adapted based on Biswakarma (2008)

Taking into mind the low representation of different caste and ethnic groups in state affairs, the government passed an ordinance in 2009 approving a law for reservation quotas for women, Janajatis, Madhesis and Dalits in the public service, including civil service and Nepal Army. The state have introduced the fourth amendment of Local Self-governance Act in 2010 and reserved 45 per cent reservation for the marginalised people. Considering this 45 per cent as a whole, Madhesis share 22 per cent, indigenous nationalities 27 per cent, women 33 per cent, Dalits 9 per cent, disabled people 5 per cent and the people from backward regions share 4 per cent.[18]

Demanding inclusiveness in state apparatus and concerning low representation of Madhesi people in Nepal Army, Madhesi political parties are demanding proportional representation of Madhesis in Nepal Army. They are insisting mass recruitment of Madhesis in it. The mass entry of Madhesi people into Nepal Army is agreed even in the Four-Point Agreement between the United Democratic Madhesi Front (UDMF) and the UCPN (M).[19] But security analysts and non-Maoist political parties are not supporting the mass entry because of the sensitive nature of the army institution. The security force, political and security analysts have not opposed the principle of inclusive nature of the army and proper representation of Terai-Madhes. However, they argue that it has to be accomplished through due process which could take several years.

Nepal Army has its own say regarding its inclusiveness. It claims that it has already a Madhesi battalion named Naya Sabuj Gan. Taking the need of inclusion seriously, it claims to have already started inclusive recruitment before the government reservation provision. It writes that it has 6,196 Madhesis from the total 92,000 armies. Among the Madhesis, 55 are officers.

Table 7 Candidacy for different post in Nepal Army

Caste	*Candidates applying for Sipahi (recruit)*	*Percentage in Total*	*Candidates applying for officer*	*Percentage in total*
Brahmins/Chhetri	8435	53.3	3683	73.8
Janjati/Indigenous people	4872	30.9	1124	22.5
Dalit	835	5.3	110	2.7
Madhesi/Tharu	1683	10.6	76	1.5
Total	**15,825**	**100**	**4993**	**100**

Source: Official website of Nepal Army[20]

Table 7 justifies the claim of Nepal Army. It is based on the new recruitment announced in 2007. For the post of Sipahi, only 1683 among 15,825 applicants were Madhesis which is just 10.6% of the total. There were 76 Madhesis out of 4993 candidates for officer's post. Referring to the low recruitment and representation of Madhesis, Nepal Army clarifies that the Madhesi youths are not much interested in joining the army. They are especially interested in technical jobs in health, agriculture, forestry, engineering etc. Moreover, most of the applicants in Nepal Army cannot pass written exams. This fact shows the need for enhancing education level in Madhesi youths for a larger enrolment rate. Besides, there is absence of the sense of belongingness in Madhesi youths towards the Army. It may be because of the feeling of inferiority or lack of ownership to the institutions or other many factors. So, the problem is equally structural as much as it is socio-economic.

Yet, we can find the recruitment of Madhesis higher in Nepal Police. Table 9 shows the recruitment since May 2006 to April 2008 in Nepal Police. It depicts that all together 1578 Madhesis were recruited in Nepal Police that is 26.2 per cent of the total recruitment.

Table 8 Recruitment in Nepal Police (May'06-Apr'08)

Caste	*Number of Recruitment*	*Percentage*
Dalit	308	5.1
Janjatis	646	10.7
Madhesi	1578	26.2
Women	439	7.3
Others	3058	50.7
Total	**6029**	**100**

Source: Ministry of Home as cited in UNDP (2009)

Due to the reservation provision and changed political scenario, representation of the excluded and marginalised groups could increase over time. Regarding the reservation provision, the chairperson of Nepal Madhesi Civil Servant Forum says that the state has declared reservation and promised not to discriminate on the basis of caste, ethnicity colour and language. But the reservation just for the sake of reservation would not increase Madhesi representation in state affairs. He further argues that the reservation seats can easily be accessible to those well competitive and talented Madhesis, who are often come from well-off families. It is a new phenomena of elite capture. But the less competitive and less talented Madhesis, who are in real need, may not get access to such reservations. Yes, reservation is one of the achievements of awakening Madhesi people and their movement of 2007. However, there exists greater risk than the opportunities for now.[21]

The government has taken initiative to make state bodies inclusive by providing reservation. But it has categorised various caste and ethnic groups under one single regional identity as 'Madhesis'. For sure, this will benefit the high caste and well-off

Terai-Madhesis from reservation and it would be unjust to the low-empowered Madhesi caste people, Madhesi Dalits and ethnic minorities. So, the small groups are demanding special reservation within the Madhesi identity. The polarisation is growing because the small ethnic and religious groups have fear of elite capture over the resources and opportunities as it is happening in Terai-Madhes since long time. This fear should be analysed in the context that the UNDP Human Development Report-2009 has shown that Madhesi Dalits have 0.209 educational attainments and 0.383 Human Development Index (HDI) level. Other Madhesi middle caste groups hold 0.330 educational attainments and have 0.450 HDI level. But the elite upper caste Madhesi have best position over all Nepalese people. They have 0.701 educational attainments and 0.625 HDI level. This difference not only symbolises the variation of capability of different caste and ethnic groups within the Madhesi community but also falsifies the blanket generalisation of Madhesi leaders that say all Madhesis are exploited. Government should take care of all these social hierarchies, communal factors and different empowerment indices while providing opportunities for the Madhesi community. Otherwise, the reservation would be grabbed by all the upper caste people and elites. It would further widen the gap between different Madhesi caste groups. Further, it will fuel the caste and class conflict within the Madhesi communities. The issues now coming on surface are not only the problems of present; they are equally the opportunities for future to make inclusive Nepal and also inclusive Madhesi communities. Reservation within reservation and social inclusion is only one way to correct social rupture. It might take some time but would definitely increase the participation of marginalised groups in every state apparatus by bringing all the ethnic and caste groups in mainstream.

2.7 Economic distribution and development disparity

The people in southern plain of Nepal have been frequently showing their dissatisfaction on budget allocation and expenditure. This region is the backbone of national economy as it contributes more than two thirds to the gross domestic product (GDP) (Shah

2006). But the government investment in this region is not satisfactory in comparison to the tax and revenue collected from here. Investment in some infrastructures has been significant but the focus has been on developing regional transaction rather than serving local population. Writings of Yadav (2007) and Gupta (2010) insist that the infrastructures are built rather to attract the migration from the hills than to serve the local people. Such an interpretation is not only partial but also misleading. Referring to the government's annual report on per capita budget investment of 2006/07, Gupta (2010) writes that the per capita budget allocation for the people in this region is lower than that for the hill people. Due to the lack of sufficient budget and development programme, Terai-Madhesi, in a collective comparison, has lower human development index than the people of hill communities (Shah 2006). However, UNDP (2009) report shows a sharp contrast against this.

Resource distribution in the past might have been unequal based on geographic areas in face value. While searching the reason macro-economically, we can find some reasons such as a) low population density, b) high cost of development projects in hills and mountains, and c) per capita investment cost due to which per capita budget allocation and expenditure might have seen higher in hill and mountain districts. This is one of the analyses of the context, but only this reason may not justify the geographic disparity in resource allocation. Initiations should also be there to address such an imbalance soon. The point to argue is that the imbalance should be calculated and compared not in a simple arithmetic way, but in a comprehensive and scientific way that could take socio-economic and geographic reasons into account.

There are 48.4 per cent of the total population residing in the 20 Terai districts. Similarly, 39 hill districts houses 44.3 per cent of the total population, and the share of the total population in 16 mountain districts is 7.3 per cent. CBS (2001) shows the population density in Terai is 329.59 whereas those in hill and mountain are 167.11 and 32.57 respectively. It shows lower population density in hills and mountains which also means that the per capita expenditure goes automatically higher when the population is scattered in difficult geographies. But the government seems not to be complying with the fact that Terai-Madhes may need more resources given the increasing population density there.

While talking about resource distribution, one should also not forget that the cost of development project is higher in hill and mountain districts than in plain districts. Due to difficult geography, scattered settlements and difficulties in transportations, hill and mountain district always have comparatively higher cost for the same kind of development projects. For example, in Terai, it costs 5 million for the construction of one kilometre gravel road. To do the same work in hill and mountain, it costs 10 million and 15 million respectively (Shah et al. 2010). One Kilogram of normal rice in Terai costs around Nepali Rupees 32 (about 0.5 USD) but in hill and mountain it obviously costs higher than that. For any kind of development project, a contactor can easily get labourers and other necessary materials in comparatively cheaper price in Terai-Madhes. These all comparable advantages should also be taken into mind while comparing the general financial statistics. Just looking at the face value does not provide the reality of political economy of resource distribution.

The demand of budget on the basis of revenue collection might be attractive for popularity but not realistic. According to the Consolidated Financial Statements of Fiscal Year 2005/2006, there are only 11 districts in Nepal which have revenues greater than the regular expenditure (total expenditure covers regular expenditure plus development expenditure) (Financial Controller General Office 2007 and 2008). Among them, eight districts are from Terai-Madhes and the rest three are from hills. In such a condition, demanding the budget allocation on the basis of revenue collection is futile. These all facts show that economic distribution and resource allocation is the matter of managing the state, not an emotional issue. This also gives indications of complications in managing/allocating resources in federations in the future.

Although the per capita expenditure is higher in hill and mountain regions than in Terai-Madhes, there are considerable disparities in development indices. Terai-Madhes having lower per capita expenditure is found better in position in different development indices such as poverty deprivation index, socioeconomic infrastructural development index etc CBS and ICIMOD (2003).

Table 9 shows that even though the per capita expenditure is high in hill and mountain regions, they are unsuccessful in holding better position in human empowerment indices. Overall on different empowerment indices, Terai-Madhes lag behind in social empowerment index. But it has better position than hill and mountain regions have on the rest of the empowerment indices including the other sectors such as health, literacy, infrastructures, poverty and deprivation measures.

Table 9 Empowerment index by region, 2001

Regions	*Social Empowerment Index (SEI)*	*Economic Empowerment Index (EEI)*	*Political Empowerment Index (PEI)*	*Human Empowerment Index (HEI)*	*Relative Value = 100*
Terai	0.362	0.392	0.674	0.476	103
Hill	0.476	0.310	0.568	0.451	97
Mountain	0.315	0.236	0.526	0.359	78

Source: UNDP (2004)

Although there might be some cases on which Terai-Madhes does not hold good positions, but the above discussion shows that Terai-Madhes is not marginalised and excluded in all matters as presented by some writers such as Gupta (2010) and Yadav (2007). There are many districts of Terai which hold comparatively better positions on development indices. There are some districts like Rautahat, Mahottari, Sarlahi, and Siraha which have extremely low development indices, which need significant attention from the state. Except these four districts, all Terai-Madhes districts lie within top 30 districts of Nepal whereas, among 16 mountain districts, only one lies within the top 30. In hill region, only 13 districts among the 39 lie on top 30 rank (UNDP 2004). So, the logic that Terai-Madhes is exploited in all sectors would just be an unscientific roar given the precarious conditions in the rural areas of hill and mountain region. In some way, poverty, deprivation and backwardness have been a collective fate of Nepalis, not only of the people from specific regions.

2.8 Proxy reasons for exclusion and discrimination

Above-mentioned six issues are regularly and strongly raised by Madhesi leaders and activists (Yadav 2006b; Yadav 2007; Gupta 2010; Gupta 2006). They strongly blame the state's behaviour of discriminating and excluding Madhesis. But only few scholars have tried to find some hidden factors within the Madhesi community that have also played significant role to keep Madhesi people backward and live in poor condition.

Of course, it is true that the government had excluded and discriminated the people in Terai-Madhes since long. But there are two other reasons that forced Madhesis to be so. The first is the social hierarchy and structure of Madhesi community, where caste/class and ethnic discrimination, gender violence, dowry system, exclusion and other social taboos. The second is the indifference to the Terai-Madhesis and their socio-economic problems by the regional leaders till the uprising in 2007.

Altogether there are 59 caste and ethnic groups in Terai-Madhes. Among them, Tharus share the largest number (21.13%) followed by Muslims (13.38%), Yadav (12.33%) and Teli (4.19%). Only these four groups are majority and hold 51 per cent of the total Madhesi population. Other caste groups are Chamar, Koiri, Kurmi, Dhanuk, Mushar, Dusadh/Paswan/Pasi, Sonar, Kewat, Brahmin, Baniya, Mallah, Kalwar, Hajam/Thakur, Kanu, Rajbanshi, Sudi, Lohar, Tatma, Khatwe, Dhobi, Nuniya, Kumhar, Danuwar, Haluwai, Rajput, Kayasth, Bandhai, Santahl/Satar, Jhangar/Dhagar, Bantar, Barai, Kahar, Gangai, Lodha, Rajbhar, Bin/Binda, Bhediyar, Gaderi, Nurang, Tajpuriaya, Chidimar, Mali,

Bengali, Dom, Kamar, Meche, Halkhor, Punjabi/Sikh, Kisan, Koche, Dhuniya, Jain and Munda and Kuswadiya/Patharkata, all these remaing caste groups hold 49 per cent of Terai-Madhesi population but neither of them exceed more than 5 per cent.

Table 10 Caste-wise distribution of development indices

Caste/ ethnicity	*Life expectancy at birth*	*Adult literacy*	*Per capita income in USD*	*Life expectancy index*	*Educational attainment*	*Income index*	*Human development index HDI*	*Rank*
All Brahmin/ Chhetri	62.95	63.65	2027	0.633	0.522	0.5022	0.552	5
Hill Brahmin	68.10	69.93	2395	0.718	0.586	0.5301	0.612	3
Hill Chhetri	60.61	58.40	1736	0.594	0.471	0.4763	0.514	9
Terai/Madhesi/ Brahmin/Chhetri	63.89	83.80	2333	0.648	0.701	0.5257	0.625	1
Terai Madhesi other caste	61.94	41.85	1119	0.616	0.330	0.4031	0.450	15
All Dalits	61.03	38.02	977	0.601	0.292	0.3804	0.424	18
Hill Dalits	60.89	45.50	1099	0.598	0.349	0.4001	0.449	16
Terai Madhesi Dalits	61.26	27.32	743	0.604	0.209	0.3348	0.383	20
Newar	68	68.20	3097	0.717	0.558	0.5730	0.616	2
All Janajatis excluding Newar	62.91	51.67	1405	0.632	0.410	0.4410	0.494	12
Hill/mountain/ Janajatis	63.61	53.81	1490	0.644	0.427	0.4509	0.507	11
Terai Janajatis	61.55	48.11	1224	0.609	0.383	0.4180	0.470	13
Muslims	60.99	30.32	890	0.600	0.238	0.3648	0.401	19
All Janajatis including Newar	63.33	53.52	1697	0.639	0.427	0.4726	0.513	10
All hill Janajatis including Newar	64.15	56.23	1869	0.652	0.448	0.4887	0.530	7
All hill mountain groups with Newar	63.12	58.47	1846	0.635	0.471	0.4866	0.531	6
All hill mountain groups without Newar	62.86	57.75	1699	0.631	0.465	0.4728	0.523	8
All Terai/ Madhesi								

groups with Muslim	61.59	42.34	1094	0.610	0.335	0.3993	0.448	17
All Terai/ Madhesi groups without Muslim	61.69	43.74	1143	0.612	0.346	0.4066	0.455	14
Other	66.35	57.97	2227	0.689	0.469	0.5180	0.559	4

Source: UNDP (2009)

A scrutiny over the human development index, as depicted in Table 10, interestingly shows that some Terai-Madhesi upper caste groups have better human development index than overall Nepalis. The UNDP Human Development Report 2009 reveals that Terai-Madhes Brahmins and Chhetris hold the highest human development index (0.625) where hill Brahmins and Chhetris have only (0.552). The Terai-Madhesi upper caste people's HDI is amazingly higher than that of the middle caste and lower caste Dalit and other backward community. The middle caste Terai-Madhesi people have 0.450 HDI, whereas the lower Terai-Madhesi caste and Dalits have only 0.383 HDI value.

Being in the agricultural country, Nepalis have to rely on land for livelihoods; it signifies power, prestige and property but most of the lower caste people or Dalits in Terai-Madhes are landless. Extremely skewed land ownership is a glaring indicator of inequality in Terai-Madhes. Due to the low representation of Dalit and backward community in political parties, their voices are not heard properly. Landlessness has been such a problem that 44 per cent among them do not have even one inch of land for livelihoods. The deprivation is comparatively higher than that of the hill Dalits (15%) and backward people.[22] According to three years interim plan (2008/09 to 2010/11), 58.5 per cent are landless in Santhal, Jhagad, Kisan and Munda communities. Similarly, 45.8 per cent of Rajbamsi (Kochi), Gangai, Dhimal, Tajpuria and Meche, 40.4 per cent of Muslims and around 79 per cent of Musahars are landless (Jha 2010).

Most of these low caste people work as tenants and agricultural labourers for the local landlords. They have limited access to food and they continue to carry an uneven burden of poverty and live in perpetual food insecurity leading to under-nourishment, high level of morbidity, lower life expectancy and higher rate of infant mortality. Unequal land distribution have made poor people's lives hard that is resulting into conflict and promoting violence. Thus, landlessness has been a perennial and prominent source of social, ethnic and political conflict Nepal (Upreti 2008). However, these issues have never been an agenda of any Madhesi regional parties. Terai-Madhesi parties have not taken any initiative from their side to solve the landlessness problem of Madhesi Dalits (Cheah 2008), rather they blamed governments for everything (Jha 2010). There is another reason that the major three Terai-Madhesi parties – the MPRF, TMDP and SP–are led by upper caste of Madhesi community. Most of them are the elites and landlords (Cheah 2008), a situation that delays the structural transformation. So one of the major hindrances for the socio-economic transformation of the poor and marginalisation of the people in Terai-Madhes is the resistance of the regional leaders, most of them representing the regional elite group, to transformative land reform as well as their inaction on untouchability, feudal practice in the name of agricultural slaves (Haliya, Haruwa and Charuwa), and patronising attitudes.

Due to being within minority, lower caste people are not respected well by the political parties. Along with this, they have low literacy rate in comparison to other Madhesi caste groups which has further worsened their situation. About 79 per cent of the Dalits, 68 per cent of Muslims, 54 per cent of indigenous Janajatis and 42 per cent of mid-caste population are illiterate (Jha 2010). The literacy rate among the Dalit and Muslim women is below 11 per cent. Worst is the literacy rate among Musahars which is seven per cent. Poverty is one and social discrimination the other factor for this kind of low literacy. Economic and social barrier to primary education has a noticeably devastating impact on their higher education. More to it, caste-based discrimination has affected the access of Dalit children to get education. This is validated by the fact that Dalits comprised only 0.8 per cent of the people who passed the diploma level in 2001 while Brahmins and Kshatriya accounted for 66.7 per cent in this criterion.[23] Dalit children face 'social discrimination' even from the discriminatory physical infrastructure and social environment at schools. Schools are typically located far from Dalit communities and in many schools, Dalit students are forced to sit at the back of the classroom. They face discrimination as 'untouchables' by both teachers and non-Dalit students. It is resulting into higher drop-out rates (Thapa 2009). However, such issues do not trigger attention of the regional leaders. The deplorable condition and exclusion of these backward castes have given birth to ethnic militarisation and rise of numerous armed groups. The coming chapters have discussed them in detail.

Gender discrimination is also a serious issue in Terai-Madhes region. Due to the high patriarchal culture, the enrolment of girl students in Madhes is lower and freedom for women is also congested. Although Madhesi people have comparatively good access to health post and hospitals than the people in hill and mountain regions, people believe more on shamans and witchcraft. It is affecting human health in general and maternal-child health in particular. Besides, the social rules and obligations have constrained empowerment of women specifically. UNDP (2004) writes that a cycle of discrimination, thus, begins with cultural and religious taboos and culminates in their reinforcement, perpetuating and deepening both poverty and inherited stigma of inferiority. Such issues have also gone unnoticed by the mainstream parties or the ones who claim to genuinely represent Terai-Madhes.

One of the major reasons behind the unequal development and empowerment in Terai-Madhesi community is its leadership. The Terai-Madhesi political leaders have been in the cabinet so many times. They frequently demand to share power; but very few times has the voice of the poor Terai-Madhesi caste groups been their issues.[24] This ignorance might have taken place also because of the electoral politics. Since the small caste groups in Terai-Madhes constitute low population, they may not be a 'good' vote bank for the political leaders. Especially, the issues of Terai-Madhesi Dalits, who pitifully fall in the lowest back in every empowerment count, have not been raised; if raised, have not been properly discussed. Hence, the lower caste and backward communities in the region are twice excluded, first by the state and second by their birth for which they are called 'low caste'. The Terai-Madhesi parties advocating for inclusion have paid apt attention to the social, cultural and religious variation in their region. Interesting is the fact that the decision-making level of such parties are mostly populated by either upper caste or middle caste elites. The way that the upper caste Madhesi leaders work suggests that they worry whether other caste groups of Madhes threat their existing domination in the parties. Report from International Crisis Group also suspects that the Terai-Madhes leaders might have seen the development of other caste groups nothing more than future challenge and threat to their own caste group (ICG 2011). It is the result of deep-rooted feudal culture in Madhesi society which is reflected in caste-based politics in Terai-Madhes.

Concerning role of Madhesi parties in Madhesi issues, their fragmentation and their insufficient effort to solve Madhesi issues, the editor of weekly magazine 'The Voice of Madhes', Rajesh Ahiraj, said that the state and Madhesi political parties both are equally responsible for the awful condition of Madhesi people. The state is responsible for the structural discrimination. Further, the Terai-Madhesi political parties with the majority of upper caste elites have always been limited to fullfill their own vested interests using the feudal characters in Madhesi society. Indeed, they are the landlords who exploited Terai-Madhesis. After joining politics, they have always bargained for seats in government in the name of poor and marginalised people by making strong critique against the state. Ahiraj further said that the Terai-Madhesi parties and government both are guilty for the deplorable condition of general Madhesi people. In such a condition, there is soaring chance of birth of new critical power in Terai-Madhes that will finish the future of these parties, and the state have to pay its cost of ignorance, if the situation continues like this.[25]

Misrepresentation or mis-utilisation of the power as representatives is another issue. Sukhdev Shah writes that from history to till date, there are fewer instances of Madhesi leaders who are recognised for putting up their Madhes agenda ahead of personal interests.[26] It is hard to believe how any of the existing Madhesi parties can claim to be serving Madhesi people's interests when they do not raise critical concerns of the Madhesi people. On the contrary, they seem to be working on cross purposes, attempting to undermine and overcome each other. It is not hard to see that Madhesi leaders are divided in ideologies, castes and regions so as just to protect their arrogance and self-pride. Dr Ram Dayal Rakesh has also written that this kind of fight among Madhesi leaders and fragmentation of Madhesi parties are just for the personal greed and vested interests, not for the benevolence of the general Terai-Madhesi people.[27]

Dissatisfaction in the Terai-Madhesi people on their leaders has begun to surface nowadays. During the focus group discussion conducted by the authors in Janakpur, Saptari and Rajbiraj, local people said that the achievement of the popular uprising in 2007 have been limited within the Terai-Madhesi politicians. They got more seats in the government; it benefited only the leaders, mostly from the upper caste. The structural marginalisation inside Terai-Madhesi community is yet to be addressed. Yes, addressing exclusion and discrimination does not need the physical presence of the people from certain communities. It is the fulfilment of essential needs and services of the people from those communities. In this context, it would be better to conclude this chapter by referring to the opinion on inclusiveness from an interview with a farmer in Morang. He had said, "*I am farmer, my livelihood is dependent on farming. I need fertilisers and other equipments on time for my farming. If a leader of my constituency can not facilitate me and alike farmers to get them conveniently on time and do not raise the issue of land reform to solve landlessness problems of thousands of Terai-Madhesis, then how can that s/he represent my voice in the state? Only being a person from my community does not mean that s/he represents me. My voices, basic needs and my rights should be kept safe in the Constitution. Only then me and alike people can feel and enjoy inclusion; but it does not matter to me whether a hill-origin or a Terai-Madhesi whoever leader does so.*"

End note

1. Prithvi Narayan Shah (1723–1775), King of Nepal, is considered to be the political unifier and initiator of modern Nepal.
2. The Khas are originated from the mountain and hill dwellers who used to live in the southern lap of the Himalayan range in Asia and later spread eastward gradually. Physically feature of them exhibit fair complexion with generally tall or medium height and mostly a long nose.
3. Sukhdev Shah was Nepalese Ambassador to the US from February to May 2009.
4. See http://archives.myrepublica.com/portal/index.php?action=news_details&news_id=27278; retrieved on 2011-01-18.
5. Panchayat system, the partyless governance, in Nepal was enforced in 1962 which continued till the 1990's popular movement overthrew the system curtailing the powers of the King and establishing multi-party democracy.
6. Interviews with local people in taken with Madhesi at Janakpur, most of interviewee are found highly concerned about these issues.
7. Sukhdev Shah as cited in Miklian (2009, p 4).
8. The Shiwalik Range is the geologically youngest east-west mountain chain in the southernmost Himalayas.
9. Some Terai-Madhes districts Banke, Bardiya, Kailali, and Kanchanpur were under Indian control. Later, East India Company returned it to Nepal in appreciation of the service of Nepali Gurkhas in supporting India's independence movement. These districts were called as New Nepal or Naya Muluk.
10. The election to the Constituent Assembly (CA) opted two ways for representation, First-Past-the-Post and Proportional representation.
11. Based on the interview with an Indian citizen who took citizenship certificate recently from Janakpur, Nepal. The name of the interviewee is not revealed due to his personal request. He admitted that he has two citizenship certificates and will use them as per his conveniences in either country.

12. *The Rising Nepal*, 18 April 2007.
13. For detail, see http://hem.com.np/2006/12/02/opponents-claim-the-new-citizenship-act-could-turn-Nepal-into-fiji/ accessed retrieved on 28 February 2011.
14. For details, visit http://www.usip.org/publications/violence-terai-region-and-Madhesi -movement-prospects-peace-Nepal retrieved on 24 March 2011.
15. http://www.telegraphnepal.com/opinion/2011-10-20/nepal-problems:-influx-of-indians-and-acquiring-citizenship-cards retrieved on 20 October 2011.
16. General Secretary of Terai-Madhes Democratic Party (TMDP) Mahendra Raya Yadav demanded an investigation into the distribution of citizenship certificates citing that the non-Nepalis were the ones mostly benefited by the distribution. For details, see *Gorkhapatra National Daily* of 7 January 2008.
17. National Education Planning Commission Report as cited Gaige (2009).
18. Nepal Gazette, Volume 60, 3 May 2010, No. 3, Part 3, Government of Nepal, Ministry of Local Development. The backward regions cover Achham, Kalikot, Jajarkot, Jumla, Dolpa, Bajhang, Bajura, Mugu and Humla.
19. The agreement was reached to form a coalition government under the prime-ministership of UCPN vice-chair Dr Baburam Bhattarai.
20. http://www.nepalarmy.mil.np/inclusiveness.php retrieved at 19 October 2011.
21. Based on interview taken with Binod Kumar Singh, Chairperson, at his office of Nepal Madhesi Civil Servants' Forum at Anamnagar, Kathmandu on 17 August 2011.
22. Three year Interim Plan (2008/09 to 2010/11)
23. Three year Interim Plan (2008/09 to 2010/11)
24. Conflict Study Center (2008) "Geopolitics of Madhes: Ballot or Bullet in Nepal!" Situation Update 62.
25. Interview taken with Rajesh Ahiraj at office of 'The Voice of Madhes' at Hanumansthan, Anamnagar, Kathmandu on 1 August 2011.
26. Sukhdev Shah, End of Madhes Debate, *Republica National Daily*, 18 January 2011.0
27. Nepal's Madhesi leaders are very shrewd, selfish and dishonest to their own people (Undated interview with Dr Ram Dayal Rakesh in *Telegraph Nepal*).

3

The Context of the Uprising

Though the people in Terai-Madhes had been raising voice against the state prejudices since 1950, the voice had not occupied as much space in politics as it has done recently. Politicians time and again used and misused the term 'Madhes' to raise local issues since about 1947 (Malla 2010). But such efforts are frequently termed as dubious as they concentrated more around electoral campaigns for vote-games and grabbing position for power and resources.

Critical concerns of identity and inclusion emerged after the restoration of democracy in 1990. To their sadness, the issues were again overshadowed because of the negligence of political decision-makers especially the Terai-Madhesi leaders as well as the disturbance of the Maoists' armed insurrection in Nepal. Though inclusion was one of the major agenda of this insurgency that claimed over 16,000 human lives, initiatives could not be taken as everything that counted was the war, frequent peace-talks and formation and deformation of the governments.

Terai-Madhesi people had been feeling excluded and marginalised for decades, especially in terms of recognition. Discrimination and humiliation went to its optimum as Terai-

Madhesi people were treated unfairly in the capital and the hill areas, especially in state mechanisms. Even amidst this perilous dissatisfaction, the state did not try to look at the issues of Terai-Madhes seriously. In 2006, Nepal ended the decade-long armed conflict, and in 2007 it went into being Federal Democratic Republic officially. It overthrew even the king transferring sovereignty of the state to the people legally. The state introduced Interim Constitution in 2007. It was silent on federalism and equitable electoral system (ICG 2007). Such silence fuelled the already heated dissatisfaction and became main reasons for the rise of the decisive uprising in 2007.

A series of political events triggered in January 2007. Showing dissatisfaction with the lack of explicit mention to the federal system in the Interim Constitution, Madhesi People's Right Forum (MPRF)[1], one of young political parties, torched it in public. It demanded an amendment in the provision of federal state and electoral constituencies. Some of the MPRF activists were arrested on the charge of torching the Constitution. To counter it, MPRF declared Madhes strike concentrating in eastern Terai. While participating in the strike, one of the MPRF activists was killed by the Maoist activists during the encounter between these two parties. Because of the government's inefficiency to deal with the situation, the protest geared up to its maximum. It started from the eastern region, especially from Siraha and Saptari districts, and spread to the whole southern plain. It continued for 21 days and claimed the lives of 29 people (Gautam 2008).

The major demand of the Madhes movement was the declaration of 'Ek Madhes, Ek Pradesh' (One Madhes, One Province) under the federal system of governance. It demanded regional autonomy with rights to self-determination. Proportional representation in the CA was also another demand. Some others were the easy provisions to acquire citizenship certificate and end of the discrimination in hiring Madhesi people in national administration, army and civil services. Later, this uprising was calmed down after signing a Twenty Two-point Agreement by the government and the unsatisfied parties (see Annex 3).

3.1 Violence during the uprising

The uprising in Terai-Madhes in 2007 escalated because of the circulation of sensational audio-visual and communalisation for political purpose. The people participated with hope that they will get dividends in the form of address to the exclusion and discrimination. But the uprising quickly burst into unlawful activities such as intentionally targeting hill-origin communities. The protesters blamed the hill-origin people as the exploiters and colonisers in Terai-Madhes. There was a mass demonstration against the hill-origin people and the state. The main slogan of this protest demanded hill-origin people to be out of Terai-Madhes. The protesters attacked many shops and houses that belonged to hill-origin people. Property worth millions was looted; houses and shops were destroyed and burnt. Hill-origin people and Madhesi protestors clashed in some places. The government became unable to enforce law and security.[2] More to it, different Madhesi armed groups carried out criminal activities as a strategic pressure. Kidnapping and asking for ransom, murder and looting the land and property of the hill-origin community increased. Due to such incidences, large number of hill-origin people felt insecure in Madhes. The environment of mistrust and suspicion between these two communities spread all over Terai-Madhes. Enmity between communities grew faster and violence escalated thereby. The following points discuss some reasons for the escalation of violence during the uprising.

- The alleged scandal in Nepalgunj, on 26 December 2006, played catalystic role to make Madhesi aggressive towards hill people. Interim government was formed after an agreement held between the Maoist and the Seven Party Alliances (SPA). But due to some dissatisfaction, Sadbhawana Party called Madhes strike on 25 December 2006. Cadres of this party were moving around the city of Nepalgunj with bamboo sticks and iron rods in their hands. Except some hotels around hospitals and nursing homes, almost all the cities were shut down. The hotels around the hospitals never used to be closed in such strikes as the relatives of patients used to have foods there. But the cadres of the Sadbhawana Party that time paid no care to this local reality. They vandalised the hotels owned by hill-origin people. They shouted the slogans against the hill-origin people and demanded them to be ousted from Terai-Madhes. They even vandalised microbuses which was on the parking. On the next day, some businesspeople, school and college students started protest against this incident. Then, this group shouted the slogans for Madhesi people to be ousted from the whole country. They also vandalised shops, houses and industries owned by Madhesi people. Like this way, the whole city was in fire by the noon (Gautam 2008).

- The whole of the protest was documented and the videos were circulated across the Terai-Madhes. This was shown in mass. In the video, several people in police dress were seen siding with the hill people. They were firing at Madhesis. They were seen destroying shops and throwing furniture of Madhesi community into fires. The footage contains sections of the crowd saying "Nepal Police Jindabaad"[3]. The persons seen in the video were in half uniform of police with their faces masked. Another line contained in the footage includes: "This shop belongs to a Nepali[4], don't destroy it".[5] Even if it is not clear that whether they were the genuine policepersons or the disguised vigilantes, the video tape was deliberately produced to escalate the violence and shown to public during the uprising. As a result, Madhesi people became aggressive against the hill people and the government and communal conflict escalated. Madhesi leaders used the contexts of the video as a means to mobilise Madhesi people.
- Different parties in then government gave controversial speech about the uprising. They blamed it as 'conducted by the royalist, vigilantes' group, criminals and Hindu fundamentalists' (Hachhethu 2007 and Mathema 2011). All of them underestimated the possible serious communal

tension. Madhesi leaders also tactfully used the response of political parties to advance the protest.

- The outgoing Prime Minister Late Girija Prasad Koirala's refusal to accept the demand of the uprising fuelled tension at first (Miklian 2009, p. 6). The refusal of demand had been interpreted as a bias from hill people-led government against the Madhesis. As a result, communal feelings erupted more among the Madhesi mass. For Madhesi leaders, Girija Prasad Koirala was not a Madhesi despite of the fact that his family was there since generations.
- Different hill-origin leaders from the Maoist party including its chairperson Pushpa Kamal Dahal 'Prachanda' blamed MPRF leaders as criminals (Mathema 2011). Dr Baburam Bhattarai blamed that hooligans from neighbouring states of India were hired to carry out the movement (Pathak and Niraula 2007). This broke the belief of Madhesi people on Maoists and hill-origin leaders.
- Madhesi activists mercilessly vandalised the property of hill-origin communities forced hill-origin people to stand in counter to the violent activities.
- Media was also heavily criticised by for the activists. Madhesi protesters threatened different FM stations not to broadcast programmes in Nepali languages.
- The protesters broke down statues of Kings, those of ancient poets in Nepali language and martyrs.[6] Such trends alienated ordinary hill-origin people in Terai-Madhes.
- Madhesi protesters torched Nepali 'Dhaka Topi' (a traditional cap worn by hill people that used to symbolise Nepalese nationalism) during the uprising.[7]

All these activities created horror, feeling of injustice, suspicion and misunderstanding in the people. Madhesi leaders tactfully used this emotion and sentiment in the uprising. Communal hatred rose to its height. Clashes between communities were frequent. Madhesi mass strongly denied the presence of hill people which was a humiliating experience for the latter. The fraternity that existed since years geared down immediately to almost null. Anarchy, uncertainty and dissatisfaction took over the previously present peace.

End note

1. The MPRF was established in 1997 and was initially registered as a non-governmental organisation. In April 2007, it was registered as a political party in Election Commission. Details can be found via http://www.satp.org/satporgtp/countries/Nepal/terroristoutfits/mjf.html; retrieved on 04 May 2011.
2. Interview taken with the hill people of Janakpur on 12 February 2010
3. English translation: 'Long live Nepal Police'.
4. In this sense, a person from hill.
5. Based on the video watched by the authors.
6. *Himal Khabar Patrika*, 30 January 2007.
7. For details, see *Nepali Times*; 'In the central and eastern tarai: Rage, determination, and grief'; 2 February 2007.

4

Reasons for the Prolonged Conflict

Terai-Madhes unrest had taken birth as a result of combination of the state's inefficiency to bring all the ethnic/indigenous and class groups into national mainstream in one hand and injection of communal divide by the Madhesi leaders and Madhesi intellectuals on the other. Although the 1990's Constitution of Nepal guaranteed equality and inclusion, only the handful of population enjoyed its fruit. Caste, class, gender, religion, ethnicity and even regional discrimination continued. Terai-Madhesi leaders continually participating in the successive governments did not work to implement the constitutional provisions to address the problems of Terai-Madhes. Though the popular movement of 1990 abolished autocratic Panchayat system and restored multi-party democracy, only the elites enjoyed most of the opportunities. The democracy exercised in Nepal seldom portrayed the ideology 'For the people, by the people and to the people'. As a result, Maoist insurgency erupted. Maoists raised the issue of race, ethnicity, language, geographic exclusion and marginalisation. They distributed the hope of rectification of longstanding discrimination, election to the CA and reconstruction of the state. These hopes help woke up the hidden and suppressed feelings of all marginalised and excluded groups. Shaking hands with the people from different communities for their rights and identity, Maoists established different sister organisations on the basis of ethnicity and region. They also established Madhesi National Liberation Front (MNLF) to 'work for' Madhesi people.

Most of the districts from Terai-Madhes were comparatively safer than hill areas during the ten years of insurgency. That is why many displaced people from hills are found settled in this region. Terai-Madhes significantly came under threat and insecurity after Jay Krishna Goit, previous chief of MNLF, left Maoist party and began armed struggle. He established an underground armed outfit named Janatantrik Terai Mukti Morcha (JTMM). Following the popular uprising of 2007, proliferation of armed outfits and their criminal activities spiralled up. Nothing but violence grew up on the fertile southern land. Some of the reasons behind these and their effects are described in the coming sections.

4.1 Rise of communalism

Sen (2006) has opined that the sense of identity can not only be a source of pride and joy but also a cause of conflicts. This duly applies in the case of Nepal's Terai-Madhes. Since 1950s, different Madhesi political parties were in struggle. They raised the issues of rights to citizenship, proportional representation and language. Due to the fight with the hill-dominant government, bond between Madhesis and non-Madhesis became fragile (Bhattachan 2008). However, people in the ground kept on saying that the relation was not so bad. Despite the political tug of war, some people still say there was mutual understanding between the communities at the local level.[1]

The violence during Madhes uprising germinated the seed of hatred between the two communities. Even though the protest was violent, Madhesi activists claimed that their protest was peaceful. They chanted humiliating slogans particularly against the hill-origin community. Their aggression was considerable. It forcefully tried to establish the fact that all hill people are responsible for the discrimination against Madhes. The protestors vandalised the property of innocent hill-origin people. Madhesi people made the slogans demanding to push out the hill-origin people from Madhes. Clashes occurred between these communities in some places. They gave birth to communal antagonism. The state mechanism did not take these series of event seriously in terms of preparing farsighted plans to address the problem, neither did the Terai-Madhesi leaders act responsibly in such a crisis. The academia took it just as a result of the systematic exclusion of the Madhes by the state (Hachhethu 2007) and failed to project early warning. Such increase in communal hatred started to make people's life insecure. Slow response of the state over the communal violence gave birth to disbelief in Madhesis towards the hill-people led government. Also, the trust of hill-origin people to Madhesi leaders sharply eroded and the gulf of suspicion further widened. Madhesis began to think that the government was not going to fulfil their demands. It further widened distance between hill-people and Madhesis. Not only these two extremes, but also the locally residing indigenous Tharus and Madhesis began to feel insecure from one another. Tharus began to see threat from the Madhesi demands (Mathema 2011 and Miklian 2009) because some Madhesi leaders and activists strongly denied the separate identity of Tharus. They argued that Tharus are the Madhes-ethnic people, like Rai and Limbu are the hill ethnics (Gupta 2010). It is claimed that Tharu language is not independent rather it is highly influenced by other language like 'Bajjika'[2]. Some other Madhesi activists also deny the existence of Tharu language stating that "there is no language named as Tharu; rather it is a mixed language of Madhesi languages" (Jha 1993). Gaige (2009: 17) states that "Tharu, although categorised by the census as a separate language for simplicity's sake, is not a single language. Tharus appear to speak dialects of the languages spoken around them". But Chaudhary (2007) has defended Tharu language and presented counter-arguments. He has explained about the scattered Tharu settlements. He has also claimed that they might have adopted different language in different places. He mentions about the archaeological evidence of a holy book Gurubabak and some other evidence found in Dang that has proved Tharus as the original and native inhabitants with a separate language. For a community to be indigenous as per the governmental requirement, it should have separate language and traditional culture and should not lie on Hindu hierarchy system. So, Chaudhary argues that the state's declaration to Tharus as indigenous people also certifies them as indigenous people with distinct language.

Thus, in Terai-Madhes, people of one community believe those in others as an actual or a potential source of threat to one's interests, values and existence. Some causes that escalated communalism are described as follows:

4.1.1 Confusions over federalism

The Interim Constitution-2007 has announced the country as a Federal Democratic Republic. Different models of federalism are under discussion thereafter. Some national and regional parties are demanding federal states as per their interests. Madhesi regional parties have claimed that federalism was the outcome of the uprising in Terai-Madhes and UCPN (M) has claimed that it is basically their brainchild. But, the opponents of federalism such as Chitra Bahadur KC argue that federalism is imposed by foreign powers. Even within the supporters of federalism, the divide is very sharp on the nature of federalism - ethnic versus non-ethnic. UCPN (M) lobbied for ethnic federal structure during war time with a targetted strategy of winning heart and mind of ethnic groups. Even after the election to the CA, this party is strongly advocating for the ethnic model of federalism. CPN (UML), CPN (ML), Nepali Congress and many other parties are in favour of non-ethnic federalism to be based on (a) identity (ethnicity/caste, language, culture, religion) and (b) capability. However, CPN (UML) and Nepali Congress are also under tremendous pressure from their own ethnic members to go for ethnic federalism. Even the CA members from ethnic groups of major parties formed caucus to establish ethnic federalism. Similarly, the CA Committee on State Restructuring, with a simple majority vote, has presented the concept of 14 federal provinces of which most (10) are based on ethnicity which suffered from sharp controversy within the CA.

On the other side, the strong demand of One Madhes, One Province raised by Madhesi leaders has further added complications. Finally, the situation is that majority Madhesi CA members, at least in public, stand behind One Madhes, One Province; many of the ethnic CA members do so for ethnic federalism and other CA members favour non-ethnic federal structure. Hence, the CA is still unable to unanimously decide federal structures. In the Interim Constitution-2007, there was a provision of State Restructuring Commission (SRC) to assist the CA to decide on federal structures. However, political parties did not form SRC bearing that SRC may propose different federal structures than their interests. Ultimately, to prevent possible case in court against non-action of the constitutional provision, political parties formed a nine-member SRC by sending party representatives as 'experts'. This was also the reason why the SRC members were themselves divided according to the position of their parties consequently producing two different reports. The regional parties on the other hand used One Madhes, One Province as a bargaining tool to acquire power. Hence, the federalism debate in Nepal is shaped by biases, revenge and retaliation, short-sightedness, emotion and interests of international actors instead of looking at the future and addressing to the most weaknesses. Hence, radicalisation and misinterpretation (e.g., interpreting ILO 169: the Right to Self-determination as separation of the part of the country), revenge (Brahmin, Chhetri and few other castes controlled the state power in the past so ethnic groups should do the same now) and biases dominate the discussion on federalism.

Figure 2 Proposed federations by majority (above) and minority (below) members of the SRC in 2012

Source: Ekantipur news portal

With the strong demand of 'One Madhes, One province', minority hill-origin people and indigenous Tharus in Terai-Madhes are found worried about their rights. This fear deepened when ethnic parties like Chure Bhawar Ekta Samaj (CBES) and Tharu Welfare Assembly (Tharu Kalyankarini Sabha) claimed of possible discrimination in Terai-Madhesi states (Mathema 2011). Minority hill and indigenous people are afraid of being marginalised in upcoming federal system. This kind of confusion over federalism is found as one of the sources of the misunderstanding among ethnic communities in Madhes.

4.1.2 Mistrust on leaders

Millions of property was lost during the violence in Terai-Madhes. More than this, the great loss of this conflict is the mutual trust between Madhesi and non-Madhesi communities. It has implanted seeds of perennial communal conflict. The overt or covert tension between the communities has deepened due to the frequent attacks of armed outfits that especially target the people of hill-origin.

Terai-Madhes-based politicians could have played significant role to minimise the communal conflict. These leaders should have assured Terai-Madhesi people to fulfil all their right demands to calm the conflict. But without playing role in peacefully settling the issues, most of these leaders were fuelling ethnic tensions, sensationalising issues and promoting hatred against hill-origin people. By setting the politically-biased history of the plain land, the leaders and activists challenged the identity and presence of hill-origin people as well as that of other indigenous people such as Tharus and Rajbamshis in Terai-Madhes. The regional parties put the demand of 'One Madhes One Province' with Right to Self-determination. The 'One Madhes, One Province' demand is neither the principle of federalism nor physically feasible. It is exactly the same unitary model of Nepal. However, Madhesi leaders are reiterating it. Therefore, the non-Madhesi communities such as Tharus and hill-origin people suspect this demand as an Indian interest planted through Madhesi leaders.

The regional leaders were busy in giving controversial speeches against hill community and the state's sovereignty. Once Upendra Yadav, the MPRF leader, said, "We would like to be governed by ourselves now. If the government does not respect our demands, we will be forced to divide the Terai region from Nepal."[3] This kind of speech completely divided the society into Pahadi and Madhesi. As a result, the number of violent clashes increased. Sadbhawana Party head Rajendra Mahato also stated, "We will wage the structure of one Madhes one province, with no alternatives; we will not allow Pahadis to rule us."[4] He also did not hesitate to state that they would join hands with the Madhesi underground armed groups if needed.[5] Similarly, chairperson of Terai-Madhes Democratic Party, Mahantha Thakur, was found seriously questioning on national integrity when he said that if one Madhes one province is not granted, then existence of one Nepal is impossible.[6] Speeches against the hill-origin community became first slogans in Madhes politics. Such statements further fuelled communal tension and eroded the trust of hill origin people on Madhesi leaders.

Different Madhesi leaders gave threat to secessionist move for the reason of which then Defence Minister Sharat Singh Bhandari had to resign from the Baburam Bhattarai government in October 2011. On the occasion of India-Nepal seminar in Vanarasi, Jay Prakash Gupta had said, "The Kathmandu rulers are cheating Madhesi people. [....] there should be group recruitment of Madhesis in the army". At last he said, "Jay Madhes! Jay Nepal!! And Jay Hind!!" while he was a representative of the Government of Nepal.[7] Many people viewed such expressions from Madhesi leaders as their efforts to make India happy to provide support to establish themselves. Tharus and the hill-origin people in Terai-Madhes are already suspicious about the alignment of Madhesi leaders with India to get support in their demand of 'One Madhes, One Province'.

Madhesi leaders refused the identity not only of the hill-origin people in Madhes but also of the indigenous Tharus. They have time and again denied the separate identity of Tharus in Terai-Madhes. Even the first Vice-President of Nepal had come under controversy after a speech on Tharus. He had once said "Tharus are no different than Madhesis".[8] And MPRF leaders even did not hesitate to say that they would teach Tharus a lesson [*will take revenge*] in future.[9] Such verbal wars are time and again fuelling tension and deteriorating the situations further.

Not only Madhesi but also non-Madhesi leaders were not able to minimize the conflict. Non-Madhesi leaders' statements on Madhes uprising also could not flourish fraternity. The Seven Party Alliance (SPA) government, which was in power during the uprising, and most of the government's shareholders were opposing the demand of single and autonomous Madhes state. Then Prime Minister Late Girija Prasad Koirala had argued that separating

Madhes as an autonomous state would split the country. He had stated that fulfilling the demand of creating whole Madhes as one state is not possible by any means (Miklian 2009). The Maoist and Communist Party Nepal-Unified Marxist and Leninist (CPN-UML) had released a joint statement on 27 June 2008 firmly rejecting the 'One Madhes' proposal as their stand.[10] Madhesi leaders treated these responses as anti-Madhesi. Hence, they oriented Madhesi people accordingly which created mistrust of Madhesis people towards the non-Madhesi leaders active in national politics. Thereafter, these non-Madhesi (hill-origin) leaders who used to win elections from Madhes were blamed that they just looted the Madhesis. So as to calm down such hatred, both Madhesi and non-Madhesi leaders should have promised for justice in future. No matter whatever the demands may be, the settlement should have been sought on the basis of all-party justice and equality. Sadly, that did not happen. Ultimately, both regional and national political leaders lost trust of the people which was risky for political stability.

4.1.3 Increasing violence and crime

Due to weak security system and unstable politics, the number of Madhesi armed outfits is increasing day by day after the uprising of 2007. According to a special report by Ministry of Home Affairs, the number of such outfits has reached to 109.[11] Among them, 107 are operating in Terai-Madhes region (Lee 2009 as cited in Mathema 2011). These armed groups were formed mostly by taking the advantage of weak transitional security situation for profit, revenge, and notoriety (Upreti 2009). Further, open border with India not only helped the armed groups to bring domestically made small arms but also facilitated choosing India as a safe hiding place.

The social harmony between Madhesi and hill-origin people is further worsened by the criminals as they mainly targeted hill-origin people in extortion and kidnapping. They have threatened hill-origin people to go away from Madhes. It was widely reported in the media that Madhesi leaders were supporting the armed groups for their activities in the name of 'One Madhes, One Province'. It has created a big question about the future of minority people in the upcoming federations. On the other side, these armed groups have geared up criminal activities targeting the hill-origin people. Different armed groups are kidnapping and killing government employees of hill-origin. These activities are making the hill-origin people feel insecure in Terai-Madhes. Terrors of frequent attacks have also forced them to be displaced. In such a scenario, many hill-origin families have been displaced from Terai-Madhes. Due to the lack of proper registration system of Internally Displaced Persons (IDPs), the displaced people from this conflict are registered nowhere. So, there is another complication in determining their exact number. But, given the situation, it is safe to say that a large number of displaced people from Madhes conflict are now residing in Kathmandu, Biratnagar, Chitwan, Hetauda and in the towns close to east-west highway such as Bardibas, Hariwon and Lalbandi etc.[12]

Even if some good progress is there at macro-political level in terms of addressing the issues such as exclusion and discrimination, the local woes are not healed yet. Due to insufficient attention from or wrong approach of the state, armed groups are brainwashing Madhesi poor people to join the outfits. Petty crimes, thuggery, kidnapping, looting, murdering, bombing and extortions are still a regular story of the people in Terai-Madhes. While the scenario is keeping on getting worse, the government (sarcastically with many Madhesi ministers including Deputy Prime Minister and Home Minister responsible for law and order at present) still have not properly planned to address the conflict. To address insecurity, the successive governments brought Special Security Strategy (SSS) to counter the crimes in Terai-Madhes. However, Madhesi leaders opposed this. It was over politicised and was ultimately foiled. A prominent example is the Special Security Strategy brought by then Home Minister Bhim Rawal at the time of Madhav Kumar Nepal government. But Madhesi leaders vehemently opposed its implementation. Though government security may control crimes, but the rift between Madhesi and non-Madhesi communities can not be bridged by such physical means. Further, the government mechanisms and representatives are absent in many of the Terai-Madhes villages due to security threats from the armed groups. Public insecurity and violence have made people's life hard.

It is said that 'Justice delayed is justice denied'. The people in Terai-Madhes are still hoping for something from the leaders from all political parties. But if their hope is not addressed in right time, it could erupt as a perilous result in near future.

4.1.4 Security dilemma

Security dilemma is one of the reasons for the ethnic conflict in the world (Wolff 2006). The essence of the security dilemma is that an increase in one person's, group's or state's security is at the same time perceived as a threat or decrease in security by another actor (ibid: 73). It is noteworthy in the context of Terai-Madhes conflict in Nepal. The formation of armed groups on ethnic and caste basis has made the society unsafe. Attack of one armed group creates security dilemma for others. By the fear of being attacked by Madhesi armed groups, hill-origin people feel security dilemma. The formation of CBES[13] and its association with military wing Chure Bhawar Shanti Sena as defensive force can be taken as the result of such dilemma. People's belief on the government security system has so much reduced that different pro-Pahadi armed groups such as Ajingar and Ex-dinosaur have been established in the name of defence from Madhesi armed groups (Pathak and Uprety 2010).

Formation and counter-formation of armed groups has fuelled communal violence. The number of clash between ethnically militarised groups is increasing. One instance here is enough to view the whole scenario. In an interview, a human right activist revealed that due to the murder of cadres of CBES by JTMM-Goit, Chure Bhawar Shanti Sena declared war against the latter.[14] In eastern Madhes, once the situation between Madhesi and Tharus was worse, Tharus and Madhesis could not endure one another groups; they used to begin fighting (Guneratne 2009). Tharus had also militarised their cadres to defy the Madhesi demands and counter the attacks.[15] This led Terai-Madhes badly fall into ethnic militancy. Fear of attack from other militarised troops, fear of being dominated by other ethnic groups and rise of counter demands compelled to think about one's own security (Housden 2009). In this way, insecurity and counter-militancy created security dilemma and prolonged the conflict.

Often media report that various armed groups active in Terai-Madhes are nurtured, mobilised and protected by Madhesi leaders for their political benefits.[16] Further, political parties created their militant wings that promoted militarisation in the society and facilitated criminal activities.

The approach of Ministry of Peace and Reconstruction has also helped increase a number of armed groups. This ministry invites armed groups for talks without any criteria. So, small groups which are organised locally by collecting few domestic arms become nationally recognised once they sit with the ministry in talks. Media coverage and news makes them popular and spread their influence locally. So, there is also a hidden motive to organise armed groups, create local terror, sit with peace ministry for talks and get legitimacy from the state. They all consequently help small local armed groups involve in violence and get national recognition.

4.2 Effect of communalism

Madhes conflict has brought significant changes in the relationship among different ethnic groups within Terai-Madhes. The first effect of the growing communalism is the alienation of Madhesi and hill-origin communities from one another. A strong and exclusive sense of belonging to one group can, in many cases, carry the perception of distance and divergence from the other groups (Sen 2006). At the present context, the feelings of being Madhesi have taken Madhesis away from the hill-origin people and vice versa.

Different ethnic groups were unsatisfied with the government for the exclusion and discrimination against them. However, communities had good relationship with each other. Social harmony and understanding between the hill-origin and the Madhesi people were at considerable. As Sen (2006) has said, a society would not take a long time to convert peace zone into conflict zone, if one discards the others' presence. The Madhes uprising and its aftermath converted the existing harmony into communal hatred. There appeared a dividing line between ethnic communities. It destroyed peace and mutuality between the communities. In this case, the sense of being Madhesi or hill-origin kept people away from each other. Thus, an environment of mistrust clouded the society. Suspicion percolated everywhere. Observations still show that communal harmony has been much worsened. Even a personal debate does not take time to be the reason for clash between communities.

Significant changes have occurred before and after the uprising. In Madhesi minority places, Madhesi people used to get invitation for the participation in social welfare programme before the uprising. But after the series of despiteful events, such mutuality has decreased. In places where they are in minority, Madhesi people have been excluded from the membership of different groups such as mother's group, community forest users' group and small cooperative groups. This is also the same for hill-origin people wherever they are in minority. Those who have already become member are less responded in the programmes. In politics too, the people from the other community are less responded by the hill-origin leaders and cadres. The situation has been such bad that every Madhesi are thought to be the follower of MPRF and are called as 'Forums'.[17]

In this way, minority Madhesis feel insecure in the places where hill-origin people are in majority and vice versa. Most of the Madhesis in minority say that the relation was harmonious before the uprising. But such an alienation generated by communalism is paralysing social relationship. As the situation has changed, they opine that the issue of rights and inclusion has been like a curse to them even though it was a major demand during the uprising.

4.2.1 Militarisation in Madhes

After the study of the history of Madhes movement, one can find that the present combative revolution and militarisation is not new for Madhesi politics and its struggle. In 1956, Raghunath Thakur had established 'Madhesi Mukti Aandolan' to fight against the discrimination and exploitation against Terai residents (Pathak and Uprety 2009). He used to argue that Terai came under Article 73 of UN Charter[18] and it was an autonomous region. Terai also had every right to make its own foreign policies (Nayak 2011). He later formed 'Madhesi Janakrantikari Dal' to continue the protest. Its major objectives were:

- to snatch power from Nepalese government for self-governance
- to choose capable Madhesis to make their own army, police and bureaucrats
- to hold domestic and international trade of Madhes to Madhesi people
- to enforce law made by Madhesis in Madhes
- to give every Madhesi land's ownership to Madhesi people, and
- to chase away all the enemies who had hold authority on Madhes (Pathak and Uprety 2009).

In Sixties, Thakur had also lobbied with different leaders of India to have his say and popularise his movement (Nayak 2011). There was the formation of another group in the same time. It was the 'Terai Liberation Front' formed to end the discrimination and exploitation against the indigenous people in Western Terai. Fighters in this Front used to carry arms against the discrimination. They had started an armed revolution like guerrilla war strategy (Pathak and Uprety 2009). It is said that many organisations had revolted with or without arms against the atrocities of central rulers. But these kinds of active combative revolutions were not seen after the end of Terai Liberation Front till Maoist insurgency.

After the ten-year long insurgency, peace process started following the Comprehensive Peace Agreement (CPA) between the government and the rebels. As per the agreement, the weapons of the Maoists are kept under the surveillance of a special committee now. However, mishandling of some weapons is reported frequently in the media. There is a rapid proliferation of armed groups after the uprising of 2007. Many groups are seen protesting either in violent or non-violent way against the Kathmandu-centred government and the hill-origin community.

The UCPN (M) first introduced the issues of ethnicity in the politics in Nepal. It raised the issues of race-, ethnicity- and language-based exclusion and marginalisation. It distributed hopes of elimination of longstanding discrimination, demand of election to the CA and restructuring of the state. Through this, the party gained strength and support from all excluded and marginalised groups. This is how it became popular and spread all over the nation (Whelpton et al. 2008). During the insurgency, the party had established different organisations based on ethnic and regional identities. MNLF had been established under the command of the Jay Krishna Goit in 2000. He left the party with his follower blaming that the Maoists are not serious on Madhes suffering. He established JTMM, an underground outfit in July 2004. Later on, JTMM was again fragmented by Jwala Singh in August 2006 (Mathema 2011). One additional case: a Platoon Commander of Maoist party, Shambhu Prasad Yadav alias Ajaya, was working in Solukhumbu. When one Maoist cadre killed his relative in Mahottari district, he revolted from within the party and established a new armed group named Madhesi Mukti Tigers (Paudel 2010). In this way, major Madhesi armed outfits are seen initially developed under the command of Maoist deserters.

The number of such armed outfits is growing day by day. They are highly indulged in criminal activities such as extortion, looting, murdering, kidnapping and other sorts of violence. The major targets are hill-origin people, businesspeople, industrialists, Madhesi elites and Maoists. These outfits are capturing the land

and houses belonging to these people and putting the demand of large amount of money in the name of donation. They have spread terror on hill-origin people on criminal base. They claim that Madhes solely belongs to Madhesi people; hill-origin people are not allowed to live in Madhes.[19] These different outfits have different objectives and demands. Some are demanding separate Madhes state. Some are demanding free Madhes without the presence of the hill-origin people. Some are demanding Madhes autonomous state. Some are demanding 'One Madhes, One Province' with Right to Self-determination. And, some are demanding the restoration of monarchy and Hindu state. It is already stated that 109 armed groups present in Nepal are listed by the Ministry of Home affairs.[20] Among them, interestingly, 107 are operating in Terai-Madhes (Lee 2009 as cited in Mathema 2011). Twenty militant groups among them are operating secessionist movement and more than 60 are against the hill-origin people (Pathak and Uprety 2009). These all have become nuisance to public security and communal harmony. In this context, following issues are considered the key to escalate militarisation in Madhes:

Weak security system

Following the UCPN (M)'s entry into mainstream politics from after signing in the CPA, Terai-Madhes began to become violent. Many outfits have emerged thereafter raising Madhesi issues. Among them, only few groups have political demands. Most of them are established by notorious criminals without any political agenda. However, all are claiming themselves as political outfits. The reason is the fragile transition and unpredictable politics in the country.[21] The government's inability to distinguish such outfits on the basis of political and criminal background is further worsening the situation. These outfits are frequently attacking the people and civil servants of hill-origin living in Terai-Madhes. Peoples' belief on security system has reduced because of the inefficiency of the government to permanently tackle with these outfits. For this reason, people have begun to prepare their security themselves. On the one side, hopes and sentiments are missing. On the other side, people are motivated and even forced to join these outfits for their own security reasons. Notorious activities are increasing in such a way that it can keep the achievements from the major uprising in shadow.[22] People's sentiment and dissatisfaction over the state have been fertile ground for the armed groups. Hence, crimes are filling the vacuum created by the weak security system.

Smuggling of arms and ammunitions

The porous border between Nepal and India along the plain land of Terai-Madhes is contributing to the smuggling of arms and ammunitions. The arms smuggling channel and network established during the Maoist insurgency period (1996-2006) have not broken yet: At present, the same channel has been used by different armed outfits.[23] Anyone can buy homemade as well as sophisticated weapons in comfortable prices from the border arms market. The price range for 20 rounds Self Loading Rifle (SLR) is USD 1400-1600 (70,000-80,000 INR), for 34 rounds Sub-Machine Gun (SMG) is USD 700-800 (INR 35,000-40,000), for 10-12-18 round pistol is USD 400-1,000 (INR 18,000-50,000) and for homemade gun is USD 10-12 (INR 500-600). One of the famous and popular pistols named Three-Fifty costs around just USD 18-44 (NPR 1500-3500). In case the buyer pays extra amount, the weapons are available in home delivery basis too.[24] Most of the armed groups discussed in this section use these easily accessible weapons. More to it, the news published in Kantipur National Daily referring to the government's special security report had mentioned that, among the 109 armed outfits, more than half are carrying sophisticated weapons like Avtomat Kalashnikova 1947 (AK-47).[25] Such an easy and a cheap access to weapons have made the society unsafe. It has given strength to the crimes and ethnic militancy.

Unemployment and frustrated mass

A large number of Madhesi youths are attracted towards the armed outfits because of the unemployment and frustration.

Working as arms smuggler and joining outfits have become a lucrative job to these people.[26] Many youths are involved in making deal with arms smuggler with the hope to get huge amount of commission.

If anyone helps pass special arms across the border, s/he gets USD 125-315 (NPR 10,000-25,000) in cash according the type of the arms s/he smuggled.[27] It is also seen that most of the armed groups are established for money-making. So, such groups are fragmented time and again on the disagreement over the sharing of black money. As numerous youths are joining armed outfits to make money easily by attacking, looting and extortion, their future is already in stake. Even without being directly involved in criminal activities, people can earn money by providing information to these outfits too. Those who provide information get 15 per cent, those who are directly involved get 55 per cent and leaders of these outfits get 30 per cent of the total amount (ibid). Thus, such kind of easy job is attracting the jobless people. Such distribution channel and strategy to do this is spreading number of the supporters and informers for the criminal outfits.

There are many youths motivated by such greed to join armed groups. Uneducated and educated both types of youths are suffering from unemployment problems. Being penniless has been such a serious problem that the youths have rejoined the armed groups even after quitting them and surrendering to the police.[28] Further, after the end of the insurgency in Nepal in 2006, an understanding has been reached to integrate the rebel armies into the national army. The armed groups in Madhes are also spreading the same hope to the local youths that if they join the groups now, then they could be recruited in the national army after some negotiations. Some youths during the field observations also expressed the government's forgiveness policy as an easy reason for them to join and leave the armed groups at anytime. The government has forgiveness policy for those who surrender themselves to the security agencies. This is generating backfire and rather attracting youths to join outfits, collect money and surrender for a safe future after the mission is accomplished.

Arms competition with the Maoists

Even though the Maoists came into peace process, it was directly or indirectly involved in the uprising in 2007 and the violence thereafter. As the major armed groups in Terai-Madhes are formed by the Maoist deserters (Paudel 2010), they made their ex-partners their first target. These outfits try to reduce the influence of the Maoists in Terai-Madhes by killing or physically harming them. Such a competition for spreading and diminishing one another's influence is exacerbating the situation. More to it, the MPRF also widely spread the message that the United Communist Party of Nepal (UCPN-Maoist) itself is not an inclusive party. They blamed that it discriminates Madhesi people in party line; hence, Madhesi people should not support them. Maoist supremo Prachanda too delivered a controversial speech over MPRF blaming its cadres as criminals and Madhes movement as an act by notorious royalists and Hindu fundamentalists.[29] That speech made Madhesi people aggressive with the Maoists as well as with the whole hill-origin community. There occurred many verbal and physical clashes between MPRF activists and Maoist cadres. Such clashes decreased after a bloody, terrific and violent clash with the loss of 28 peoples' lives in Gaur massacre on 21 March 2007.

Following the CPA, the arms of Maoists are locked and kept under surveillance. However, some of the arms are allowed to be kept with Maoists personally for the security of their leaders. Some arms are reported to have been misused too. This has generated threat to the armed groups in Terai-Madhes as major of them are archrival of Maoists. Hence, the members of such armed groups almost always take weapons with them in fear of encountering armed Maoists. This is also because the fights between Madhesi outfits and Maoists are not settled yet.[30] This is why there always remain high chances of violent clashes between these groups.

During the Maoist insurgency, the government had provided arms and trainings to the Local Defence Groups. But they were not properly documented. Even after the peace agreement, the governments have not shown willingness to withdraw these weapons. This has been another catalyst for the militarisation in the post-war phase. Such trained paramilitary groups in the past have now turned into armed outfits in Terai-Madhes.[31] After such series of armed activities and insecurity, people are losing faith in peaceful progress and democracy.

Open border

Nepal and India has 1,753 kilometre open border (ICG 2007). It needs no legal documents to cross the border for the citizens from both countries according to the 1950's Peace and Friendship Treaty between India and Nepal. Anyone can easily cross the border. So, there are two most significant effects of open border along the Terai-Madhes. One, it positively benefits socio-economic exchange for the people. Many Madhesi families generally go to Indian border cities for daily shopping as goods are cheaper in Indian sides. Indian cities are easily accessible for study and jobs also. So, people prefer to go to such cities than to Kathmandu.

The other effect is alarming that the open border is misused by the criminals. Large number of criminal groups has taken benefit of the open border. It is also accused that there was a large mass of Indian people infiltrated for a specific purpose in Madhes uprising allowing the border to play vital role in making the unrest successful (Pathak and Niraula 2007). Armed groups have made Indian states their operational base. Border has become an easy gateway to safe haven after committing crimes in Nepal. Due to the weak security management, smuggling and bootlegging are increasing around the border area. The open border is not only misused by Nepali criminals but also by the outsiders. ICG (2007) reports that improvement of the security in Bihar (the adjacent Indian state) has forced Indian criminals to displace their operating bases to Nepal. Moreover, Indian citizens are also involved in different armed outfits either as trainers or as weapon suppliers.[32]

Due to the open border, Indian people have also established armed outfits to operate in Nepal. The huge sarcasm is that they operate in the name of Terai Mukti (liberation of the plain land in

Nepal) and perform criminal activities.[33] The open and ineffective management of border have made easy access to weapons too. So, reaching an agreement over properly managing or controlling border is essential for to strengthen security situation in Terai-Madhes.

4.2.2 Effect of militarisation

Forced migration

Among different consequences of Madhes uprising, one is the massive displacement of hill-origin people from Terai-Madhes. It has also become a significant cause for the changing relationship between the communities. A number of people were displaced from Madhes districts. Reasons of such displacements can be categorised in three folds: 1) victimisation and threats to evacuate the region by the Madhesi outfits or activists, 2) fear of potential attack and harassment from the Madhesis and 3) minorisation, terror of the possible tension after federalisation.

The first type of displaced people had almost already left Madhes without selling their property. But the second and third types of people have been leaving Madhes after selling their property in far cheaper price than the real market value. According to their economic status and relation, these displaced people have chosen new places for settlement. A number of people have moved along the east-west highway or the towns and urban areas of adjoining (hill) districts or Chure-Bhawar areas or in the capital city Kathmandu wherever they feel safe. Paudel and Ghimire (2010) has categorised the displaced people into three categories. They are:

a. General hill-origin people
b. Government employees
c. Industrialists, businesspeople and landlords

a. General hill-origin people

This category includes those people who are living in Madhes since many generations. They are involved in shop-keeping, public services and agriculture. Most of them are well assimilated into Madhesi culture. For example, some of them have been celebrating different Madhesi festival like Chhath. Living in Terai-Madhes since many generations, they rarely have property outside Terai-Madhes. They fluently speak local Terai-Madhesi language. For instance, hill-origin people staying in Mithila areas (Mahottari, Dhanusa) speak Maithili well. During the uprising, they felt the first sense of insecurity; they had forgotten the woe suffered during the uprising. But due to frequent attacks and threats from armed groups, they are compelled to leave Terai-Madhes. People are scared of being harassed and attacked. Kidnapping of family members, unreasonable donation and confiscation of the land and other property are the remaining reasons for displacement. Many cases of misbehaviour with the hill-origin ladies by Madhesi youths have also been reported.[34]

Box 1 Double displacement

Padma Bahadur Tamang (name changed), 45, used to live in Mahendranagar, Dhanusha district after being displaced from Sindhuli by the Maoists. Now, he has settled in Bardibas. While talking about his displacement, he said "I am unlucky, I got displaced two times. First, it was by the Maoists from my origin land. I sold all the things and went to Mahendranagar. Second time, I am again displaced to Bardibas because of the conflict in Terai-Madhes. The environment of living in Madhes has been over. It is not as favourable as it was before. Frequent cases of robbery in our settlement, stealing of cattle, harassing words, chances of rape had increased. One day, one Madhesi was beaten in Hariwon. But as a result, our four innocent boys were thrashed heavily in retaliation at our settlement. Tell yourself, who wants to live there in such a condition."[35]

Source: Paudel (2010).

After this communal tension each and every personal issue of misunderstanding has been started to take communal form. If any Madhesi is beaten in hill majority places, hill people living in Madhesi majority places have to be the victim of retaliation. These minorities have become the victim of two sides. On one side, there is always the fear of extortion, robbery, rape, abduction and murder by different armed groups. On the other, rage of the Madhesi youths who are always ready to attack on them in retaliation. Due to these problems, large numbers of general hill-origin people are displaced from eastern and central Terai-Madhes.

b. Government employees

Most of the government offices suffer from the absence of the staff in the districts in Terai-Madhes. Different armed groups have threatened hill-origin employees to leave the area. These armed groups extort heavily from the Madhesi employees too. The groups allege that the capital-centred government sends its corrupt employees to suck the southern geography. Some argues it as a shadow form of colonisation. This approach of armed groups is taken as a pressurising strategy for the government to appoint the officials only from Terai-Madhes. Though this demand might sound logical at face value, but, by doing so, it might also suggest that the Terai-Madhes workers should not be appointed in hill areas too. So, exclusionary practice on the basis of regionality seems widening the rift more.

Government employees regularly get letters from armed outfits for donations. There are many murder cases due to the denial for providing donation. There are reports of a number of extortion threats on phone by the individuals and groups operating from Indian territories. After continuous threats from armed groups, many civil servants are taking prolonged leave, seeking transfer or even resigning from the post. Referring to then Minister for Home Affairs, a daily newspaper had reported that altogether 32 government employees had been killed since the gone three years

(2007-2010) in Terai-Madhes.[36] But government employees' organisations refuse this stating that the number is certainly much higher than this. Following this, the government employees resigned collectively demanding security in many places of the Terai-Madhes districts. The VDC Secretaries are serving as the representatives of the government and also acting as heads of VDCs since a decade as the term of locally elected representative expired. But now they have moved to district headquarters and threatened to resign en-mass if the government forces them to go to their assigned villages. The single reason they are citing is the security threat in Terai-Madhes only because they are of hill-origin.

According to OCHA's Nepal Situation Overview in 2009, government offices of eastern and central Terai-Madhes are found vacant. It states that around 90 per cent of government offices face human resource shortage in the region. More than 40 per cent of VDC Secretaries have shifted to district headquarters due to the threats of physical attacks by underground groups. As a result, most of the offices there are without chiefs, while others face a severe lack of human resource.[37] Although the government tried to introduce stronger security system, it did not work well because of the non-cooperation from opposition parties and Madhesi leaders. The security issue in Terai-Madhes is blatantly politicised. Hence, armed groups activities and terrorism are out of control. The confidence of the underground groups is such high that they had once attacked an Assistant Chief District Officer (CDO)[38] and once demanded heavy donation even from an Assistant Minister elected from Madhes.[39] The field surveys by the authors reveal some of the following reasons behind the displacement of the hill-origin government employees from Terai-Madhes:

- Threats from different armed groups and Madhesi activists
- Humiliation by the Madhesi co-workers.
- Fear of being attacked by the Madhesi activists on the blame of being corrupt and insincere towards Madhesis.

- Demands for huge amount of donations.
- Feeling of insecurity and loneliness due to the displacement of large number of hill-origin employees.
- Misbehaviour by Madhesi youths to the hill-origin ladies (their family members) and inefficacy of police action against the wrong-doers.
- Family pressure to leave the place.

Some hill-origin government employees have shifted their family from Terai-Madhes cities to the cities with the majority of the hill-origin people whereas they still work in Terai-Madhes cities. Some of them who had properties in Madhes devaluated the price and sold immediately to shift to safer places. The sales were down to less than the half of the actual amount. The land deal became lucrative business in Terai-Madhes. It was widely observed that hill-origin land-owners did get phone calls during the nights and threatened either to immediately leave the place or face physical punishment (assault and murder etc.). Next day, the same group without revealing their identity go to the family and offer to buy their land if they sale. In such a way, the bandits and criminal gangs get the land in extremely cheap price (sometimes up to 10 times lower than the current market price). If the land-owners reject to sell, the intensity of threats would be more severe ultimately forcing the owners sell lands at any cost.

Some other people fled before selling anything. The actual number of displacement could not be acquired by the researchers due to the lack of proper registration system. Some tentative figures are available. Pathak and Uprety (2009) claims that more than 900 hill-origin civil servants, including over 700 VDC Secretaries and 200 other government staffs had fled the place. Nayak (2011) also asserts that around 300 people lost their lives in the communal and ethnic violence since 2006.

Box 2 Government employees' displacement

Shantiraj Baral (name changed on request), 33, is a government employee. He used to live in Namuna Basti Janakpur in a rented house with his family. Now, he has shifted his family to Bardibas village. When asked about the reason for displacement, he said that, "I left the city because one of the houses in my neighbour was attacked by Madhesi youths at night. Indeed, they had tried to rape the girls, but later the police filed it not as a rape but as a dacoit case. It arrested the suspected ones. But local Madhesis blamed it as a conspiracy to send their children to jail. There was almost à clash between local Madhesis and hill-people. Later, Madhesi people and parties released the culprits from police custody. After that, hill people in that area started to sell their properties to migrate. Feeling insecure, I too fled with my family. I daily go to Janakpur office with other employees by Bus. But I am always afraid of being mishandled, abducted and killed by armed groups. People generally do not like to go alone. We left to wear *Dhaka Topi*[40] also because of the fear of being harassed. There is no security guarantee to hill-origin people in Madhes."

Source: Paudel (2010).

The story in Box 2 indicates the severity of politicisation of crime based on communalism. Once crimes are politicised and criminals are protected by politicians, justice becomes non-existent. Such politicisation of crimes should be prevented at political level but the regional politicians tend to label any crimes committed by Madhesis against hill-origin people as a legitimate act to change the discriminatory practice existing in Terai-Madhes for centuries. Whether the culprit is Madhesi or hill-origin one, s/he should be under the common law. But over-politicisation according one's partisan favour is deteriorating the situation day by day.

Table 11 Name of the government employees killed by the armed groups in Terai-Madhes

S. N.	*Name*	*Address*	*S. N.*	*Name*	*Address*
1.	Nawaraj Bista	Udayapur	17.	Mohammad Husad Ali	Saptari
2.	Puran Singh Pradhan	Mahottari	18.	Shiv Prasad Sharma	Nawalparasi
3.	Rajkumar Joshi	Dhanusha	19.	Kumar Niraula	Janakpur
4.	Ram Babu Sharma	Bara	20.	Sunil Yadav	-
5.	Prabhu Narayan Yadav	Saptari	21.	Bashudev Paudel	-
6.	Ram Brichha Ray	Rauthat	22.	Raj Kumar Joshi	Dhanusha
7.	Manohar Kumar Shrestha	Birgunj	23.	Barun Bahadur Jaiswal	Sarlahi
8.	Arun Kumar Shrestha	Siraha	24.	Purna Prasad Dhakal	Banke
9.	Nagendra Prasad Yadav	Mahottari	25.	Bikram Shah	Saptari
10.	Karna Bahadur B.K.	Sarlahi	26.	Ram Milan Gupta	Kapilvastu
11.	Suresh Kumar Yadav	Rautahat	27.	Alaudhin Ansari	Mahottari
12.	Jitendra Prashad Sah	-	28.	Ramhari Pokharel	Siraha
13.	Mohan Prasad Mainali	Parsa	29.	Bindheswor Mahato	Sarlahi
14.	Narayan Khadka	Birgunj	30.	Ganesh Bahadur Shrestha	-
15.	Shrawn Kumar Shrestha	Janakpur	31.	Lok Nath Gaire	-
16.	Mukunda Prasad Khanal	Birgunj	32.	Narendra Khati	-

Source: Naya Patrika National Daily, 24 February 2011

c. Industrialists, businesspeople and landlords

At first, the armed outfits started demanding money from the hill people and government employees in Terai-Madhes. After the significant declination of the number of hill people in Madhes, they started to make target to Madhesi elites, landlords, industrialists and businesspeople. They did not attack these people directly but approached them first with the demand of huge amount of money. The results of denial turned into kidnapping or shooting to death. A large number of industrialists and businesspeople and their children had been attacked and kidnapped.[41] Police investigations claim that these outfits were using Indian mobile phone numbers or unregistered Nepalese mobile phone numbers to demand money. This kind of attacks to industrialists, businesspeople and landlords are still seen increasing in large cities such as Birgunj, Biratnagar and Janakpur.

The displaced industrialists, businesspeople and landlords are moving either to Kathmandu or to the Indian states. It is also found that many such displaced people have bought houses and land in Indian states. In the recent years, the displaced industrialists have established new businesses in the adjacent Indian states. Every attack on these people is resulting into the capital flight creating a serious problem in the Nepalese economy.

Box 3 Displacement of an industrialist

> One of the industrialists from Janakpur said, "This country has been totally investment-unfriendly. Here are many problems such as labor disputes on the basis of political ideology, power-cut and weak security system. Every day, we got calls from different criminal groups for donations. If we deny, they threat to kill us. The security has worsened for few years creating insecurity for further investment. One of my sons-in-law was about to establish a factory here, but due to the same problems he turned back to India to do so.

Source: Field interview, 10 February 2010

Box 3 shows the intensity of problems to the business community. In addition to extortion, the labour dispute and trade-unionism have also annoyed business community.

4.3 Rise of ethnic politics

Before 1991, the discussion on ethnic issues used to be taken as a conspiracy against the state. But now, such issues have become one of the major ingredients of Nepalese politics. Ethnic issues of the southern plain also became strong after the uprising in 2007. Regional political parties made it their major slogan. It also resulted into communal polarisation in some districts. It is moving far eyond identity politics.

Before the uprising, hill-origin leaders also used to win parliamentary elections from Terai-Madhes. But the Madhes uprising brought an unexpected change. Now, it has almost become necessary for one to be a typical Terai-Madhesi to win elections from there. It is evident from the fact that after the changed political situation, many politically and socially established hill-origin leaders in Terai-Madhes lost their vote banks and faced defeat in election against Terai-Madhesi candidates who were neither known earlier nor had social recognition before.

The voice of Madhes against the discrimination had begun to surface around 1950s. Vedanand Jha had established the first regional party (Terai Congress) in Terai-Madhes (Hyome 2006). That party demanded autonomy of the Terai-Madhes and Hindi as its lingua franca. But it did not sustain. Later, on the same way, Nepal Sadvawana Party (NSP) was established in 1985 by Gajendra Narayan Singh. At the beginning, it used to be called as Nepal Sadvawana Parishad. Later, it turned as Nepal Sadvawana Party. It had aimed at protecting the interest of the Madhesi community and providing citizenship to the people there. It had favoured the introduction of Hindi as the second national language. This party hardly won six, three and five seats in the parliamentary elections held respectively in 1991, 1994 and 1999 (EC 1999). Overtime this party is breaking down to different fringes parties and is less influential in Madhes politics. Nevertheless, some fractions of this party are always in the government since 2006.

In the history of Madhesi struggle for rights, MPRF raised the issues strongly. Its protest against Interim Constitution-2007 became the flash point of Madhes movement. Just after the uprising in 2007, many regional parties were created. Most of such parties including MPRF were created by those leaders who left the major national political parties. MPRF is basically under the leadership of an ex-Maoist leader who had revolted from CPN (UML) first and joined the UCPN (M) and then again revolted from this party also to create MPRF by bringing few leaders from Nepali Congress and CPN (UML). These leaders accused that the parties led by hill-origin people will not do favour to the Madhesi people thereby justifying their formation of new parties. By this, there were already three major regional parties (Sadvawana, MPRF and TMDP) but their splitting resulted into more than dozen of parties with less influence over the issue.

Later, three main Madhesi parties MPRF[42], SP-Mahato and Terai-Madhes Democratic Party (TMDP) collectively formed United Democratic Madhesi Front (UDMF). UDMF put the demand of single autonomous Madhes state with Right to Self-determination. It called strikes in different times. Finally, it reached an Eight-Point Agreement with the government on 28 February 2008 (see Annex 4 for the full text version of the Agreement). These three parties put the 'One Madhes, One Province' as the election slogan and gained 11.3 percent of the nationwide vote and 81 of 601 seats in CA (EC 2008, Miklian 2009).

After the Madhes uprising, the concern over the security of hill people living in Terai-Madhes grew up. It was followed by the establishment of CBES (later transformed into Chure Bhawar Ekata Party [CBEP]). This party also raised hill people's issues in Madhes. It suspected on the possible discrimination of the hill people in the possible Madhesi federal state. Then it also countered the demand of 'One Madhes, One province' with the claim of Autonomous Chure Bhawar Region. The agenda of the Terai-Madhesi regional parties and CBES were different and CBEP was the product of the ethnic pressure of Madhesi people to hill-origin people staying in Terai-Madhes for generations. CBES institutionalised its demand by signing in the Nine-point Agreement with the government (See Annex 5 for the full-text of the agreement).

Due to this kind of demands for ethnic states by regional parties, Tharus began to feel fear of ostracisation, violence and discrimination. Then, they also organised into a political unit called Tharu Welfare Assembly and started threats to create havoc in the country if the state did not immediately pay attention to their identity needs.[43] This party also demanded Tharuhat Autonomous State. That time too, the government reached an agreement with Tharus and made the rage calm down temporarily.

Whatever the agreements were, their implementation part is weak. Hence, all the previously agitating parties are now pressurising the government to follow and implement the understandings. They are sometimes threatening that they will go into protest again if all the lines of the agreements are not implemented to the fullest. Hence, the issues in Terai-Madhes need to be settled sensitively. If not, this will trigger tension from these three major forces. Politically as well as socially, the issues in Terai-Madhes are highly sensitive and dangerous if left unheard (Miklian 2009). Madhesi leaders also seem to use Madhes as the opportunity for their political survival. Often, responsible leaders are talking on sensitive issues irresponsibly. A leader of breakaway of MPRF, Mr Jay Prakash Gupta (who was often in power since 1900s political change when he was in Nepali Congress and himself a Senior Minister in the cabinet before sent to jail after the charge of corruption from the Supreme Court), threatened to separate Madhes if Kathmandu ignores his demand on Madhes. Then, on 12 February 2012, the President called the Prime Minister and warned him not to allow his cabinet ministers to speak against the national sovereignty. Against the President's stand, he wrote long justification of his statement and defended (but again from the same rhetoric). This single incident demonstrates the opportunism of Madhesi leaders that they do not act when they are in power and vomit anger when powerless.

4.3.1 Effect of ethnic politics

The feeling of ethnic hatred was fuelled during the 2007 uprising. Madhesi parties' pamphlets demonised hill people accusing them as the agents of 'coloniser'. The footage of Nepalgunj Scandal also stimulated racial discrimination. Accusations by Madhesi leaders help spiral up hostility and characterised hill people as antagonists in the mindset of the general Madhesi people. Speeches against the hill-origin community become first slogans in Madhes politics.

Miklian (2009) opines that the Madhesi parties were misusing political power to draw attention of Madhesi community. One after the other Madhesi parties is competing with each other on making stronger protest and words against the capital just to attract Madhesis in political favour. He states that Madhesi leaders are becoming popular in Madhes by fuelling ethnic division. Those who express more strongly against the hill-origin people or Kathmandu are seen as leaders supporting the cause of Madhesi marginalisation. But it is obvious that this is a faulty approach because it swippingly shift the blame to others. One of the most important causes of the marginalisations and inequality of Madhesi people are the Madhesi elites, who have not only exploited the poor and weak people but also preventing the land reform and other social reform. Such hardcore ethnic politics in heterogeneous society has made minority people insecure. As a result, a number of non-Madhesis also started to polarise in respective ethnic line. Tharu indigenous people and hill-origin people established their own ethnic parties claiming separate identity and provinces. Tharu group has claimed a separate Tharuhat and a separate identity than Madhesis have. Similarly, it is also objecting the Madhesi demand of 'One Madhes, One Province'. It has its own armed force to fight for their causes. It claims to have around 22,000 Tharu boys and girls 'ready to fight'.[44] Due to such demands, Tharus have been started to be taken as a pro-hill group by the Madhesis. Regarding such a huge fragmentation of the society Guneratne writes that if relations between Tharus and Madhesis collapse, it would lead to Balkanisation of the ethnically very heterogeneous villages of the eastern Terai (Guneratne 2009). Once Nepal's Permanent Representative to United Nations, Dr Jaya Raj Acharya, argues that the rise of ethnic conflict in Nepal can be more dangerous than the Maoist war if it is not addressed on time.[45] Lessons from former Yugoslavia, Ethiopia and North India also depict the same risks of ethnic conflict in Terai-Madhes.

There is a clear fragmentation in the society. People are resorting to ethnic, caste- and class-based organisations for individual security. Such a fragmentation was visible especially during the times of election to the CA as most of the people did not vote on the basis of political ideology. Rather they looked at whether the candidate is from their ethnic/caste group or not. In different Madhesi districts, large number of Madhesis voted the candidates from their ethnic groups rather than voting to non-Madhesis as in previous elections. Referring to the changed scenario, district members of different national parties (UCPN-M, Nepali Congress and CPN-UML) do blame Madhesi parties for playing upon ethnic spirit (Paudel 2010). But Madhesi leaders deny it. They argue that Madhesis has now become aware on choosing their true representatives. Madhesi leaders charge that these all accusations are because of the lost of vote bank by the national parties. In this way, the political leaders are in one way or the other responsible for the fragmentation of the society. Clashes between cadres of different parties (NC versus UCPN-M, CPN-UML versus UCPN-M, national parties versus Madhesi parties, and even among Madhesi outfits) along the ethnic line suggest an unsafe future of Terai-Madhes, if situation continues like this.

End note

1. Based on interviews with Madhesi and hill people at Bardibas on 10 February 2010
2. It is a type of language used in Madhes. According to census 2001, there are 1.05 per cent Bajjika speakers in total population.
3. See *Himal Khabar Patrika*, 'Chhainan Karyalaya Pramukh', 29 April 2007.
4. 'Minister Mahato's remarks spark protests', Nepalnews dot com 13 May 2007.
5. We can join hands with Madhesi armed outfits if required, an interview with Rajendra Mahato by nepalnews.com available at http://www.nepalnews.com/archive/2011/others/interview/apr/interview02.php; retrieved on 31 October 2011.
6. *Samachar Patra National Daily*, 21 December 2008
7. *Nepali Times*, 'Venting it out in Varanasi', 3 October 2008
8. 'Tharus are basically Madhesis: VP Parmananda Jha', *Telegraph Nepal*, 27 March 2009.
9. *Nepali Times*, Slow-burn in the Tarai, 08 August 2008.
10. One Madhes, One Province demand rejected, *Telegraph Nepal*, 27 June 2008.
11. *Kantipur National Daily*, Ek Saya Nau Samuhako Chirfar, 1 August 2009.

See Annex 1 for the elaborate list of the groups.

12. *Himal Khabar Patrika*, Chupchap Bisthapan, 16 December 2006.
13. This party had been registered as a regional party to participate in the election to the CA.
14. See *Himal Khabar Patrika*, Aparadh lai Rajnitiko Aawaran, 30 May 2007.
15. Republica National Daily, Tharuhat outfit trains 'army', 19 September 2009.
16. See *Himal Khabar Patrika*, Aparadh lai Rajnitiko Aawaran, 30 May 2007.
17. Madhesi people were found to be called as 'Forums' whenever the non-Madhesis had to show dissatisfaction over them in anything. The word originates from the name of 'Madhesi People's Right Forum', which is considered by the non-Madhesi people as the major responsible actor for all these conflicts. The paragraph is based on the findings of the observations and personal interviews taken intermittently in Janakpur, Rajbiraj, Bardibas, Hariwon and Lalbandi in February 2010.
18. Chapter XI of the UN Charter is about the declaration regarding non-self-governing territories.
19. *Himal Khabar Patrika*, Chainana Karyalaya Pramukh, 29 April 2007.
20. *Kantipur National Daily*, Ek Saya Nau Samuhako Chirphar, 1 August 2009.
21. *Nepal Weekly*, Bharatle Kina Maljal Gardai Chha Bikhandan Lai, 5 August 2007.
22. *Kantipur National Daily*, Madhes Bidhrohako Teen Barsha, 21 January 2010.
23. *Himal Khabar Patrika*, Rajya Chaina Madhesmaa, 14 June 2007.
24. *The Kathmandu Post*, Firearm smuggling rife in Rautahat, 27 December 2008.
25. *Kantipur National Daily*, Ek Saya Nau Samuhako Chirfar, 1 August 2009.
26. *Nepal Weekly*, Hatiyar Mohama Madheska Yuwa, 20 March 2011.
27. *Himal Khabar Patrika*, Hatiyarko Shrot, 2 September 2007.
28. *Nepal Weekly*, Antata Mohabhanga, 12 December 2010.
29. Maoist Chairperson Pushpa Kamal Dahal had publicly said that the trouble in the Terai-Madhes is because of the criminal elements. For details, see *Nepali Times*, 'State of confusion', 13 July 2007.
30. *Himal Khabar Patrika*, Rajya Chhaina Madhesma, 14 June 2007.
31. *Himal Khabar Patrika*, Pratikar Samuhako Bhaya, 14 March 2008.
32. An Indian dacoit Dhirendra Yadav was one of the active suppliers of the

arms and ammunitions in Madhes. One of the central members of JTMM-Goit had expressed grief and indicated his arrest as a heavy loss. Yadav himself revealed at police custody that he used to supply weapons to MPRF as well as to some other outfits. For detail see, *Himal Khabar Patrika,* 'Sashastra Aandolanma Bharatiya Aparadhi, 13 February 2007.

33. Indian citizen Sukhadev Singh, a former active member of JTMM-Jwala, had later established another outfit named Terai Kranti Morcha (TKM).

34. See *Himal Khabar Patrika*, Chupchap Bisthapan, 16 December 2006, for details on severity of the displacement of hill-origin people from Terai-Madhes.

35. As interviewed on 11 February 2010 in Bardibas.

36. Nayapatrika National Daily, *Teen Barshamaa 34 Karmachari Maariye,* 24 February 2011.

37. OCHA, Nepal Situation Overview, Issue No. 50, Covering the period 16-30 June 2009 Kathmandu, 1 July 2009.

38. Kantipur National Daily, Sahayak Prajiamathi Aakraman, 12 January 2009.

39. For details, see http://www.ekantipur.com/kantipur/news/news-detail.php?news_id=11720 accessed on 10 April 2010.

40. Dhaka Topi is a type of hat. Nepalis, especially the Khas people in hills and Himalayas consider it as a pride due to its cultural attachment. It used to be widely worn by government employees and was also a part of the national dress.

41. OCHA (2009) Nepal Situation Overview Issue No. 50, covering the period 16-30 June 2009 Kathmandu, 1 July 2009

42. Later, the MPRF (Democratic) joined UDMF and MPRF-Nepal quit the front.

43. Tharu Community rejects One Madhes demand, *Telegraph Nepal*, 28 June 2008.

44. *The Kathmandu Post*, Armed squads' tribe growing, 3 January 2009.

45. Dr Acharya served as Nepal's Permanent Representative to United Nations in 1991-1994; interview taken by Mr Ramesh Koirala; for details, see http://cffn.ca/news/0708/070811-NBAInteractionNepalAbroad.pdf accessed in 12 December 2008.

5

IMPACTS OF CONFLICT

The conflict in Terai-Madhes has shown both negative and positive impacts. On one hand, it helped generate the changes and empowerment that Nepal had never seen before. On the other, it dragged a formerly peaceful and fertile land into the perennial violence. This chapter discusses some conflict-induced positive and negative changes in Terai-Madhes.

5.1 Increased participation

The post-1990 political change in general and Maoist as well as Terai-Madhes revolt in specific brought enormous awareness in Nepal. ACHR (2009) terms the conflict in Terai-Madhes as one of the least reported conflicts, which were initially overlooked, but which brought significant changes in Nepalese politics. The uprising, which started in the beginning of 2007, has turned Madhes into a strong force in Nepalese political arena. Before the uprising, Madhes was in less attention in national politics. After the uprising, the Madhes issue has become a clever political card. The national political parties used to win large numbers of seats from Madhes but in the elections to the CA, conducted in the aftermath of the uprising, but national parties lost their past stronghold and the regional Terai-Madhesi parties won 83 seats.

Madhesi leaders often contested themselves and divided instead of working together on the Madhes issues and therefore they were not able to properly represent the land in the parliament. Different factions of NSP, a Madhes-based party, used to win hardly few seats in the parliamentary elections because of their failure to concertedly work for the common purpose. There were numbers of Madhesi politicians in national parties. But as the uprising shook the ground of Nepalese politics, most of the Madhesi leaders left their former parties either to join or to form new regional parties with ambitions to be the heads of the new parties.[1]

As Madhes is a geographic region, people of any ethnic groups living there should have been called as Madhesis whether they are hill-origin residing for decades in the southern-land or the indigenous inhabitant there. Many hill-origin people residing in Madhes identify themselves as Nepali-speaking Madhesis. Many of them are residing in Terai for generations. But Madhesi leaders deny this definition. They shifted the definition of Madhes from its geographic origin to racial and ethnic identity. That benefited the Madhesi politicians in the following ways:

- There is an informal but a strong feeling developed after 2007 that it needs to be a Madhesi to win elections from Madhes areas. Hence, people can easily be deviated into ethnicity and racism in election times. It decreases the chances for non-Madhesi candidates to win elections from Madhes. This factor had great impact in the elections to the CA.
- By fuelling ethnic divisions, they whitened themselves from the previous blame of being corrupt and Kathmandu-centred. They pretend to be good politicians in the eyes of Madhesi people by making strong words against Kathmandu and hill people (Miklian 2009).

Due to rise of ethnic sentiments, people started to look caste, ethnicity and religion as the criteria to give votes. Most of the people left looking after the ideologies of the political parties. Consequently, Madhes-based parties like MPRF, different factions of NSP, and TMDP candidates bagged historic votes. NC, UML and some others lost many seats. Madhesi parties covered 83 of

601 seats in the CA (EC 2008). It became a historic representation of Madhesis in the national politics.

Box 4 Political ideology guided by ethnicity and caste

A Madhesi woman named Rama Devi (changed), 45, explained about her voting last time: "I used to be a supporter of NC party; but this time I voted to TMDP. Only Madhesi parties can understand Madhesi problems. Large number of hill people used to win elections from here. But what they did for us? They blamed our uprising as royalist and criminal activity. Those congress [Nepali Congress Party] leaders made the police shoot our men. But now we know to whom we should vote. *Beti Aur Vote Apan Jaat Mein Dev* (We give our daughter and vote to the men from our same caste, not to the others)!!

Source: Field survey on 10 February 2010

A number of hill-origin candidates used to win from many Terai constituencies in the past. For instance, in the parliamentary election held in 1999, among 88 parliamentary members from 20 Terai-Madhes districts, 43 were Madhes-origin representatives. Reason behind the winning of hill-origin political leaders from the Terai-Madhes region was because there was no such distinct ethnic divide and communal conflict. Further, some authors such as Gurung (2001, p 160) has said that "... this increase in hill dominance is due to the change in Terai social demography through migration of hill people in Madhes; hill population constitutes 30.9 percent of the population in Terai-Madhes lands". But, in the elections to the CA, most of these hill-origin politicians lost election because of fear factor, communal tension and insecurity. However, some analysts have also argued that the defeat of the hill people in Madhes is a part of the historic injustice corrected in a democratic framework.[2]

5.2 Power-centric emergence and breakdown of parties

The 2007 uprising gave a U-turn to Madhesi politicians. They accumulated never seen victory during the election to the CA. The election was conducted on two bases: first-past-the-post and proportional representation system. The following sub-section describes their major victories individually.

a. NSP-Anandi Devi

This party had launched 104 candidates in the first-past-the-post election but didn't win a single seat. Although 68 candidates were launched, the party however won two seats through the proportional representation system. The members in the CA from this party are given in Table 12.

Table 12 Name list of CA members from NSP-Anandi Devi

First-Past-the-Post	*Proportional representation*
	1. Sarita Giri
	2. Motilal Dugad

Source: EC (2008)

Later, Dugad split the NSP-A in September 2011 and formed a new party named Nava Nepal Nirman Party.[3]

b. SP-Mahato

It had launched 87 candidates in the first-past-the-post and 100 candidates in proportional elections. But it won only four from the former and five from the latter system. Later, Anil Kumar Jha split SP-Mahato and formed Sanghiya Sadvawana Party on 18 July 2011. To this date, only five CA members remain in this party.

Table 13 Name list of the CA members from SP-Mahato

First-past-the-post	*Proportional representation*
1. Rajendra Mahato	1. Gauri Mahato
2. Saroj Kumar Yadav	2. Ram Naresh Ray
	3. Laxman Lal Karna

Source: EC (2008)

Table 14 Name list of the CA members from Sangiya Sadvawana Party[4]

First-past-the-post	*Proportional representation*
1. Khobhari Ray	1. Anil Kumar Jha
2. Mahesh Prasad Yadav	2. Malamati Devi Rana (Chaudhary)

c. TMDP

The party had brought 97 candidates for proportional representation system and 94 for the first-past-the-post system in elections to the CA. It won 11 seats from proportional representation and nine seats from first-past-the-post system. On January 2011, TMDP got split, now there are only 11 CA members in this party. The remaining CA members formed TMDP-Nepal (TMDP-N).

Table 15 Name list of the CA members from TMDP

First-past-the-post	*Proportional representation*
1. Brijesh Kumar Gupta	1. Kashi Devi Jha
2. Hridayesh Tripathi	2. Kabindra Nath Thakur
3. Jitendra Prasad Sonar	3. Basanti Jha
4. Ram Kumar Sharma	4. Bimal Kumar Kedia
5. Ganesh Tiwari Nepali	5. Jay Prakash Yadav
6. Ishwor Dayal Mishra	

Source: EC (2008)

Table 16 Name list of the CA members from TMDP-Nepal

First-past-the-post	*Proportional representation*
1. Govinda Chaudhary	1. Arbind Sah
2. Sumitra Devi Raya Yadav	2. Salauddin Musalman
3. Dan Bahadur Kurmi Chaudhary	3. Chandan Sah
	4. Ramani Ram
	5. Urmila Mahato Koiri
	6. Mahendra Prasad Yadav

Source: Party office

d. MPRF

MPRF had launched 103 members for the first-past-the-post and 99 members for proportional representation system. The party bagged 30 seats from the former and 22 seats from the latter system. Later, this party also split. Twenty-seven CA members got together under the command of Bijay Kumar Gacchedar and established MPRF-Democratic (MPRF-D).

Table 17 Name list of the CA members from MPRF-Nepal

First-past-the-post		*Proportional representation*	
1.	Upendra Yadav	1.	Shrawan Kumar Agrawal
2.	Renu Kumari Yadav	2.	Madhusan Agrawal
3.	Vijaya Kumar Yadav	3.	Ram Sahaya Prasad Yadav
4.	Muhammad Wakil Musalman	4.	Rambha Devi
5.	Mohammad Istiyak Ray		
6.	Hari Narayan Yadav		
7.	Shiv Pujan Ray Yadav		
8.	Abhisekha Pratap Shah		

Source: EC (2008)

Table 18 Name list of the CA members from MPRF-Democratic

First-past-the-post		*Proportional representation*	
1.	Bijay Kumar Gacchedar	1.	Ram Janam Chaudhary
2.	Mugalal Mahato	2.	Asha Kumari Sardar
3.	Hem Raj Tated	3.	Durga Devi Mahato
4.	Sanjay Kumar Sah	4.	Ramchandra Ray Aamat
5.	Laxman Mahato	5.	Sewaki Devi Das Tatma
6.	Ramanand Mandal	6.	Kalawati Devi Dusadh
7.	Migredra Kumar Singh Yadav	7.	Lalita Shah
8.	Ram Bachan Ahir Yadav	8.	Nilam Verma
9.	Bhimrajchaudhary Rajbanshi	9.	Tilak Bahadur Rawal
10.	Karima Begham	10.	Shiv Narayan Urawa
11.	Pramod Prasad Gupta		
12.	Sharat Singh Bhandari		
13.	Kaushal Kumar Ray Yadav		
14.	Satrughan Prasad Singh Koiri		
15.	Surya dev Prasad Ojha		
16.	Om Prakash Yadav		

Source: Party office

MPRF -Nepal got split and formed MPRF-Republican (MPRF-R) in May 2011.

Table 19 Name list of the CA members from MPRF-Republican

First past the post	*Proportional representation*
1. Jay Prakash Prasad Gupta	1. Nandan Kumar Dutta
2. Rajlal Yadav	2. Chandrika Prasad Yadav
3. Raj Kishor Yadav	3. Sabita Devi Yadav
4. Akwal Ahamed	4. Shandhya Devi
5. Om Prakash Yadav	5. Surita Kumari Shah
	6. Bishwonath Yadav
	7. Atmaram Shah
	8. Salma Khatun Mikrani

Source: News agencies

e. Representation of Terai-Madhesis in the CA from different parties

The Election Commission had set a rule for the proportional representation system that a party should have enlisted 31.2 percent Madhesi candidates in the closed list.[5] Because of the regional Madhesi parties' heavy number of candidacy in the election, the national parties also had to give a number of Madhesi candidacy. This generated more representation of Madhesis also in the other national parties. Table 20 depicts representation of Terai-Madhes in different parties.

Table 20 Representation of Terai-Madhesis in CA from different parties

S.N.	*Political parties*	*First-past-the-post*	*Proportional representation*	*Total*
1	UCPN- Maoist	19	33	52
2	Nepali Congress	8	21	29
3	CPN-UML	4	21	25
4	Rastriya Prajantra Party		3	3
5	CPN-M		3	3
6	Janamorcha Nepal		1	1
7	Nepal Communist Party-United		1	1
8	Rastriya Prajantra Party-Nepal		1	1

9	Nepali Janata Dal		2	2
10	Dalit Janajati Party		1	1
11	Independent	2		2
	Total	**33**	**87**	**120**

Source: Adapted from EC (2008)

In the CA, there are 202 Terai-Madhesi representatives out of 601. It is 33.61 per cent of the total representation. It is historic as well as the largest representation of Terai-Madhesi people ever.

5.3 Mismatch between awareness and delivery

One of the great achievements of Terai-Madhes conflict is the increased level of awareness among people. This region had not been debated at this degree in terms of social and political rights, human rights and other basic rights than it has been now. Before the uprising, people were inexpressive and leaders were happy and active in mainstream politics. Nowadays, people are radicalised and political leaders are dividing them into geographic identities such as Madhesis and Pahadis to maintain their political influence. However, they lost trust of Madhesi people as they failed to constructively engage in state building. People are expecting the services and rights that they should be endowed with and Madhesi political leaders play constructive role to secure these rights. However, Madhesi leaders have not changed their feudal practices. They never raise voice on land reform in Madhes, addressing the problem of Haruwa-Charuwa and landless people. Instead, they seem to go for exclusive political control in Madhes by not being ready to provide economic rights to the landless people.

5.4 Inclusion of federalism in the Interim Constitution

Interim Constitution-2007 was amended addressing to include 'federalism' in the Interim Constitution. Some writers argue that increment and redistribution of electoral constituencies and federalism were the results of this movement (Hachhethu 2007). With increased constituency areas and changed politics, a number of Madhesis are present in the CA. Hence, it was hoped that they will constructively engage in constitution making. However, the evidences since Madhes revolt in 2007 show that they focus on capturing power and position. The split of parties one after another to go to the power is an instance to this. Nepal is in critical transition and making this transition smooth, ensuring rights of the people as well as promoting communal harmony, mutual trusts and co-existence is the tasks of the leaders. But they failed to demonstrate their leadership in this respect. The demand of 'One Madhes, One Province' that they made is neither within the basic principles of federalism nor the unanimous interests of the residents of Terai-Madhes. Tharus are heavily opposing this demand. Experts too do not subscribe to this concept. National parties are against this proposal. Therefore, the concept of 'One Madhes, One Province' is becoming a perennial source of conflict and tension instead of establishing political, economic and cultural rights of the people. It does not even fit the criteria (identity and capability) established by the CA to be federations as it completely deny the linguistic, cultural and ethnic diversities in the region and only tries to homogenise the geography as only Madhes.

5.5 Hope and frustration for dignified life

Some changes after the Madhes revolt are worth noting. Before the movement, Madhesi working class people were treated unequally in Kathmandu and other hill dominant areas. Nowadays, there is more sensitivity.[6] Madhesi working class people have begun to gain respect from others while being addressed. More to it, the first President and the first Vice-President of the country are from Madhesi community. Many ministers, members in political appointments are from Madhesi community. In the post-CPA time, Madhesi elites are the most privileged in politics. They are getting huge funds and opportunities from donors. However, for landless, homeless, the poorest and the marginalised Madhesi people, there has not been much change yet as those who claim themselves as liberators of Madhes are not only ignoring these people but also creating strong barrier by their inaction on ensuring minority

Madhesis' rights.

5.6 Ethnocentric caste politics

Ethnicity has been deep-rooted in the politics of Terai-Madhes. Previously, it used to exist in social form; but the leaders have now begun to use ethnic sentiments as a political card for their benefits. Parties have also started to be known on the basis of castes. For instance, people of other caste except Yadavs blame MPRF as a Yadavist party. Most of its party members belong to Yadav caste group which is one of the most elite caste groups in Terai-Madhes.[7] Yadavs are also blaming TMDP as groups of upper castes (Guru Jees). NSP is blamed as the gathering of landlords and businesspeople.[8] Hence, caste sentiment was heavily used during the elections to the CA. Madhesi people say that in minority Madhesi settlement areas, these leaders talk about identity of whole Madhesi community. But when they reach to Madhesi majority places, they talked about only their certain castes. They have used the caste system as vote bank politics creating binary opposition (Paudel 2010). On other side, minority caste people have established their own small caste organisations to raise their issues. However, over four years of research on Terai reveals that the elite Madhesi politicians do not take minority issues seriously and opportunistically use only for to win the elections.

Interestingly, during the election, the minority caste groups have collected fund from Madhesi candidates in return of votes. It was found that such groups had openly asked for money in return of voting. While asked during FGDs on why they followed this strategy to sell votes, they answered that the parliamentarians will not favour the demands of minority caste groups after winning the election. Hence, they better collected money to fulfil their needs. This shows a grave mistrust of minority groups towards Madhesi leaders. Indeed, ethnic and caste politics has made election system a business in Terai-Madhes again with much benefit to Madhesi elites.

Important to note, Pathak and Uprety, (2009) opine that only certain caste groups in Terai-Madhes have benefited from the movement. The caste groups such as Jha, Yadav, Singh etc. are dominant in politics and are capturing power and resources since long time. Still, the same caste groups are more at the forefront of power, politics, property and privileges in Madhes than Dalits and marginalised ones are. Dalits and backward communities were exploited by the Madhesi elites since long and this practice has not changed even after the Madhes movement of 2007. Hence, marginalised, poor, landless and homeless people from Terai-Madhes are not satisfied with the parties. They view that no existing Terai-Madhesi parties are committed to the issues of minorities and they are not inclusive in party composition too. Though the parties advocate for the inclusion of all Madhesis in state affairs, high-caste and middle-caste people dominate in all of them.[9] Hence, the frustrated minority caste groups have started to raise their identity issues being away from just Madhesis. Dissatisfaction on such minorities is growing steadily (Mathema 2011). The minority people have begun to be organised politically as they do not want to be dominated by upper caste and elite Madhesis in future. Non-Yadav intermediate castes and other backward classes want reservations and recognition as they do not see safe future under the aegis of Madhesi upper castes and Yadavs and the future federal structure.[10] The respondents during this research argued that there is no substantive difference between past and present in terms of their livelihood stress, exploitation from elites and structural inequalities. They also argued that the Madhes movement benefited a lot to upper caste elites of Madhes but did nothing to the poor, homeless and landless people as the Madhesi leaders are not willing to give power and resources to them. Now, non-Yadav leaders in different parties (Mandals, Shahs, Brahmins and others) are polarised to keep them safe from Yadav hegemony.[11] As a result, military and paramilitary groups have emerged with identity issues (Pathak and Uprety 2009). Situations show that the identity-based militarisation has become a serious threat in Terai-Madhes.

5.7 Criminalisation of the youth

Crime has become a daily nuisance in Terai-Madhes. Weapons are easily accessible. Proliferation of armed groups is spiralling. The society itself has become unsafe after the uprising. The trend of migration of the people from rural area due to insecurity has not ceased yet.[12] Armed outfits are using, abusing and misleading the youths towards militarisation. They have allured the youngsters to earn large sum of money within short period. The youth are much attracted to carry guns and other weapons. It is a human nature to exercise power; and a person having gun and money is regarded as the power factor in the society. Armed groups are persuading young boys to join them. And no doubt, it is the power that influences the system on the desired direction. Though it was difficult to confirm, some of the informants of the research, preferring anonymity, also shared that many influential Madhesi political leaders have either created or used the armed groups to fulfil their vested interests. As discussed earlier in this book too, some independent media reports also claim this to be true. Referring to the zonal headquarters of police, Nepal Weekly magazine has published that more than 80 per cent of the youths charged of carrying illegal weapons are of below 25 years merely in Narayani zone. Gun has become a part of youth culture that the youth feel proud in carrying weapons and roaming around villages in the name of armed groups. Youth involvement is found in more than 90 per cent cases of illegal weapons.[13] Hence, demographic dynamics has also become a very serious issue in Madhesi communities. Earlier study of one of the authors of this book has demonstrated that the proliferation of small arms was the product of Maoist insurgency which has been further continued in Terai-Madhes.

During the field observation of the researchers, local people also showed dissatisfaction towards Maoists and the state. There were two reasons: one is the establishment of MNLF by the Maoists, the other is the establishment of anti-Maoist paramilitary groups by the government during the insurgency period. These two groups not only spoilt the future of the youths, but also introduced the culture of sponsored violation, militarisation and revenge/retaliation. The establishment of the paramilitary groups by the government provided state-backed way to kill and suppress the opponent and institutionalised the gun culture. More to it, the government is not able to take the weapons back from such paramilitary groups even after the peace agreement.[14]

The state's weak security apparatus is one of the reasons pushing youths to join armed groups. The armed outfits' activities have been so increased that feeling of insecurity is at its height (Interdisciplinary Analysts et al. 2011). Living a life without aligning to any armed outfits has become hard in many parts of Terai-Madhes. Sending a family member to join an armed group is the only way to avoid from being looted or killed.[15] Sending one member from family to fight was first introduced by UCPN (M) during the war time. The underground armed groups followed the same approach even after the CPA.

Unfortunately, many people who have left home to join armed groups are the socially excluded and unemployed youths. Being armed has been a money-making business and thus an attraction for jobless people. Some youths have joined armed groups also to take revenge of the past with the landlords and high-caste people. In such a way, youths, who are frustrated from every corner of life, have been found taking resort to violence that helps them gain social power too (Paudel 2010).

Among the ones engaged in criminal activities, lower-caste and poor youths have the majority. Armed Police Force (APF) officers of Janakpur opine that because of being jobless and excluded from the society, the youths have chosen wrong way. These lower-caste youths used to be in the Maoist party before. But, after the peace agreement, they felt insecure being Maoists in Madhes and joined different armed groups.[16] A member from one of the outfits said, "There is no choice for us." He added, "The so-called upper-caste people exploited us; if anything wrong happened in the society, everyone did blame us and the police also used to torture us. On the other hand, we do not have job. Everywhere people either demand money or higher education if we ask for a job. We do not have both. On such a condition, what should have we done? So, we choose to be armed. Now, I am making handsome amount of money. After earning enough, I will surrender myself. There is always open door to surrender, without any cases."[17] It is the only a drop in the ocean; there are a number of such cases in Terai-Madhes.

End note

1. There are many renowned Madhesi leaders and cadres who changed their former parties, for example, Jay Prakash Gupta, Mahantha Thakur, Bijay kumar Gacchedar changed their former parties and joined or different regional parties
2. *Nepali Times*, 'We are used to the bombs. This is our chance to be heard', 11 April 2008.
3. Later, Dugad split the NSP-A in September 2011 and formed a new party named Nava Nepal Nirman Party. For details, see 'Dugad quits NSP (A), forms new party' published on 2011-09-01.
4. Based on the news report by *Telegraph Nepal* on 'Nepal Sadbhavana Party splits: Jha bids adieu to Mahato', 19 July 2011.
5. Election to Members of the Constituent Assembly Act, 2064 (2007), Certification date: 2064/3/8 (22 June 2007) An Act No. 2 of the Year 2064 (2007) enacted by the Legislature-Parliament.
6. Based on interviews with Madhesi street vendors in January 2011 in Lalitpur.
7. *Himal Khabar Patrika*, Forumka Yadavjiharu, 14 May 2008
8. Based on the interviews in the field.
9. *Naya Patrika Daily*, Samabesi Chainana Madhesi Dal, 18 January 2010.
10. Nepali Times, 'Tarai fragments', 21 November 2008.
11. Nepali Times, 'Caste aways', 26 June 2009.
12. Kantipur National Daily, 'Madhes Bidhrohako Teen Barsha', 21 January 2010.
13. Nepal Weekly, 'Hatiyarmohama Madheska Yuwa', 20 March 2011.
14. Himal Khabar Patrika, 'Pratikar Samuhako Bhaya', 14 March 2008.
15. See http://www.nepalitimes.com.np/issue/2008/11/21/PlainSpeaking/15398; accessed on 23 March 2011.
16. In Madhes, there are many armed groups formed by Maoist deserters who have made the Maoists their first target.
17. Based on the interview with Raju Sada (name changed upon the responder's request) in Rajbiraj on 10 February 2010.

6

Trend in Conflict and Security

As described in the introductory chapter, Terai-Madhes was comparatively peaceful than hill areas even during the Maoist insurgency. This region fell into an abyss of insecurity after the uprising in 2007 despite the praise-worthy socio-political change that the movement brought forward. The comparison between INSEC (2007) and INSEC (2008) shows that the frequency of killing and abduction has increased in the southern plain after the uprising. INSEC (2007) shows only four cases of killing and four cases of abduction charged in the name of armed groups in 2006 in Terai-Madhes. But in total, there were 457 cases of killing and 2006 cases of abduction in 20 Madhes districts that year. Most of the cases of abductions and killings were committed by the Maoists. The Maoists were on the lead of violation of human rights in 2006, although they had entered peace process since November that year.

Unexpectedly, even before the completion of one year of Maoists' arrival into peace process, the uprising erupted in 2007. Along with the movement, different Madhesi armed groups appeared in the name of 'liberation' of Terai-Madhes land. Armed groups got favourable environment to perform for their goals, no matter the purpose was good or bad. As a result, the cases of killings and abductions increased in 2007. Several tables in the coming pages illustrate the security situation of Terai-Madhes after the peace agreement.

Table 21 Killing and abduction in 20 Madhes districts-2006

S.N.	Districts	Perpetrator in killing					Perpetrator in abduction				
		The state	*Madhesi activists/ Armed groups*	*Uniden-tified*	*Maoist and others*	*Total*	*State*	*Madhesi activists/ Armed groups*	*Un iden-tified*	*Maoist and others*	*Total*
1	Jhapa	5	-	-	32	37	-	-	-	81	81
2	Morang	11	-	-	33	44	-	-	-	153	153
3	Sunsari	3	-	-	6	9	-	-	-	34	34
4	Saptari	2	1	-	21	24	-	1	-	99	100
5	Siraha	-	2		18	20		1		45	46
6	Dhanusha	2	-	1	17	20	-	-	-	20	20
7	Mahottari	2	-	1	8	11	—	-	-	33	33
8	Sarlahi	7	1	-	39	47	-	1	-	91	92
9	Rautahat	8	-	-	10	18	-	1	-	31	32
10	Bara	1	-	—	11	12	-	-	-	49	49
11	Parsa	2	-	-	5	7	-	-	-	833	833
12	Chitwan	22	-	-	3	25	—	-	-	18	18
13	Nawalparasi	6	-	—	33	39	-	-	-	129	129
14	Rupandehi	10	-	-	29	39	-	-	-	9	9
15	Kapilbastu	9	-	-	12	21	2	-	-	44	46
16	Dang	3	-	-	14	17	-	-	-	80	80
17	Banke	10	-	-	23	33	-	-	-	74	74
18	Bardiya	1	-	1	8	10	-	-	-	79	79
19	Kailali	2	-	-	11	13	-	-	-	51	51
20	Kanchanpur	3	-	-	8	11	-	-	-	47	47
	Total	109	4	3	341	457	2	4		2000	2006

Source: Adapted by the authors on the basis of INSEC (2007)

Table 22 shows the available data on abductions and killings in 20 Terai-Madhes districts in 2007. INSEC has not reported name of all the armed groups for different criminal activities in its report. Few armed groups are mentioned for different criminal activities of killing and abduction. This may also be the reason why Maoists and other nameless groups are seen to have greater number of such activities. Although, the total number of killing and abduction there had decreased in 2007, such crimes by different armed groups had increased in 2007. The decrease was seen due to the Maoists' arrival in peace process and their less engagement in criminal activities. In 2007, there were 363 cases of killing, of which 102 cases were committed by armed groups; the number was four in 2006. Similarly, total cases of abduction were 691 among which 331 were committed by the armed groups.

Table 22 Killing and abduction in 20 Madhes districts-2007

S.N.	Districts	Perpetrator in killing				Perpetrator in abduction			
		The state	Madhesi activists/ Armed groups	Maoist and others	Total	State	Madhesi activists/ Armed groups	Maoist and others	Total
1	Jhapa	4		11	15	-	2	21	23
2	Morang	4		25	29	-	1	8	9
3	Sunsari	3	3	6	12	-	12	19	31
4	Saptari	2	17	14	33	-	118	18	136
5	Siraha	4	10	14	28	-	57	21	78
6	Dhanusha	2	6	15	23	-	24	9	33
7	Mahottari	-	4	9	13	-	21	9	30
8	Sarlahi	5	1	24	30		8	7	15
9	Rautahat	-	39	15	54	-	69	22	91
10	Bara	6	14	16	36		7	30	37
11	Parsa	3	4	16	23	-	1	17	18
12	Chitwan	-	-	1	1	-		19	19
13	Nawalparasi	-	-	13	13	-	7	52	59
14	Rupandehi	-	3	2	5		-	28	28
15	Kapilbastu	-	1	19	20	-	2	8	10
16	Dang	-	-	3	3		2	16	18
17	Banke	-	-	8	8	-	-	16	16
18	Bardiya	-	-	3	3	-	-	6	6
19	Kailali	-	-	11	11	-	-	21	21
20	Kanchanpur	-	-	-	3	-	-	13	13
	Total	33	102	225	363		331	360	691

Source: Adapted by the authors on the basis of INSEC (2008)

The comparison of the tables 21 and 22 shows that the cases of crimes had increased in 2007. Criminal activities and human rights violation did not calm down although the state tried hard to establish law and order. Killing, abduction, threatening, beating, torturing and robbery became daily nuisance. One of the main reasons of proliferation of the armed groups and armed activities was the non-cooperation and even opposition from the Madhesi leaders against the government security plan. Madhesi leaders vehemently opposed the integrated security plan developed by Home Ministry and therefore it was not effective. Hence, politicisation of security, radicalisation of the youth (against each other group), militarisation of the society and obstruction of the functioning of the security apparatus caused grand security failure in Terai-Madhes.

The government brought Special Security Strategy (SSS) in 2009 taking into account the cases of human rights violations and crimes. It had aimed to address insecurity with the following aims:[1]

1. to deal with threats to internal security,
2. to end highway/road obstructions, abductions, extortion and other illegal acts,
3. to take action against organised crimes and lawlessness,
4. to maintain law and order,
5. to strengthen three security agencies: Nepal Police, Armed Police Force and National Investigation Department,
6. to deploy additional security personnel to contain armed activities of underground outfits and conduct swift action against them,
7. to launch an awareness programme about the SSS

Although the SSS had been brought to overrule the crime, it was criticised by different Madhesi leaders.[2] They blamed that it had been brought to make Madhesi people silent.[3] It was also blamed that the APF has increased the killing of the outfit members in the name of 'encounter'.[4] But, the security officers time and

Table 23 Killing and abduction in 20 Madhes districts-2008

S.N.	Districts	Perpetrator in killing					Perpetrator in abduction				
		The state	Madhesi activists/ Armed groups	Uniden-tified	Maoist and others	Total	State	Madhesi activists/ Armed groups	Un iden-tified	Maoist and others	Total
1	Jhapa	1	-	2	12	15	-	-	-	3	3
2	Morang	-	3	11	18	32	-	1	5	20	26
3	Sunsari	1	2	6	8	17	-	1	7	1	9
4	Saptari	9	7	21	-	37	-	48	61	1	110
5	Siraha	4	6	21	5	36	1	8	37	7	53
6	Dhanusha	4	8	-	32	44	-	17	22	6	45
7	Mahottari	1	3	8	3	15	-	32	14	2	48
8	Sarlahi	-	2	13	8	23	-	2	11	2	15
9	Rautahat	2	8	7	4	21	-	11	3	-	14
10	Bara	5	9	-	10	24	-	-	12	-	12
11	Parsa	4	5	3	4	16		-	5	3	8
12	Chitwan	-	-	1	1	2			1	24	25
13	Nawalparasi	1	4	6	6	17	-		1	8	9
14	Rupandehi	2	8	7	1	18	-	—	3	3	6
15	Kapilbastu		9	21	4	34		3	3	8	14
16	Dang	7	1	1	3	12				6	6
17	Banke	1	4		2	7		8		7	15
18	Bardiya		1		1	2		-		6	6
19	Kailali	3	-	1	4	8	-	-	1	5	6
20	Kanchanpur	-	-	-	3	3	-	-	-	2	2
	Total	**46**	**80**	**129**	**129**	**383**	**1**	**131**	**186**	**114**	**432**

Source: Adapted by the authors on the basis of INSEC (2009)

again claimed that the armed outfit members were shot death during cross-firing.[5] Different regional parties organised protest programmes against the arrest and death of the outfit members.

The special security strategy did not get support from Madhesi parties making it ineffective to contain Madhesi armed groups. Rather, different armed groups unified to strengthen their capacity to respond to it.[6] Even though there was a little decrease in crime rate, there was no expected improvement in the situation. Regional leaders and some Madhesi activists also blamed that SSS further supported armed groups and pressurised for its withdrawal.[7] However, police officers continued claiming that the security has improved in Terai-Madhes due to the SSS.[8] INSEC (2011) also endorses the police officers' claim. In fact, the cases of killing and abduction had decreased in 2009 in comparison to 2008 and 2007 (ibid 2010). Police took action to many armed group leaders resulting into the falling down of crime rate. A large number of armed militants surrendered in fear of getting executed by security forces.[9] This made general people feel relatively safer than before from communal attacks.[10]

According to INSEC (2010), the cases of killing and abduction in Terai-Madhes districts were 276 and 193 respectively in 2009. Among the cases of killing, 16 were by different armed groups, 21 by unidentified groups and 201 by Maoists and others. There were 11 cases of abduction by different armed groups; 14 were by unidentified groups and 168 were by Maoists and others.

Mostly hill-origin people residing in Terai-Madhes are feeling relieved with the improvement in security. Nevertheless, rural people in Terai-Madhes have different experiences regarding the SSS. They say that they are suffering from two sides: on one side, unnecessary torture and raid by security forces, and on the other, living made hard by armed outfits in rural villages.[11] General Madhesis opine that security forces and their tight security along the border area made them difficult to go India for regular shopping. As mentioned, cities in the adjacent Indian states are the hubs for

Table 24 Killing and abduction in 20 Madhes districts-2009

S.N.	Districts	Perpetrator in killing					Perpetrator in abduction				
		The state	Madhesi activists/ Armed groups	Uniden-tified	Maoist and others	Total	State	Madhesi activists/ Armed groups	Un iden-tified	Maoist and others	Total
1	Jhapa	1	-	1	14	16	-	-	-	3	3
2	Morang	-	-	1	12	13	-	-	-	6	6
3	Sunsari	-	—	2	10	12	-	1	1	6	8
4	Saptari	5	1	-	15	21	-	1	1	35	37
5	Siraha	2	4	1	15	22	-	2	1	10	13
6	Dhanusha	7	4	2	26	39	-	2	-	16	18
7	Mahottari	-	—	2	14	16	-	2	1	10	13
8	Sarlahi	-	-	2	13	15	-	-	2	27	29
9	Rautahat	-	2	2	14	18	-	-	2	2	4
10	Bara	1	4	1	10	16	-	1		4	5
11	Parsa	6	-	1	9	16	-	-	1	4	5
12	Chitwan	3	-	-	6	9	-	—	-	17	17
13	Nawalparasi	-	-	1	4	5	-	1	1	3	5
14	Rupandehi	5	-	1	3	9	-	-	1	-	1
15	Kapilbastu	-	—	1	6	7	—	-	1	1	2
16	Dang	3	-	-	3	6	-	-	-	4	4
17	Banke	2	1	1	11	15	-	1	1	7	9
18	Bardiya	-	-	-	3	3	-	-	1	3	4
19	Kailali	3	-	-	7	10	-	-	-	9	9
20	Kanchanpur	-	-	2	6	8	-	-	-	1	1
	Total	**38**	**16**	**21**	**201**	**276**	**-**	**11**	**14**	**168**	**193**

Source: Adapted by the authors on the basis of INSEC (2010)

local Madhesis to buy daily needs. Some Madhesi activists also show aggression against SSS.

Security officers accept that crime has not come under control even after their serious efforts. They claim that security actions are not effective as desired due to the political protection to these outfits. The security forces are unhappy for the political parties have not been supportive on their fight against the armed groups. Rather, these leaders organise protest programmes against arrested armed group members or their death in cross-firing.[12] "The problem is becoming complex and unstoppable because the issue is utterly politicised and the armed outfits' activists are getting ethnic, political and racial support; police's actions on them are taken as government suppression and discrimination against the whole Madhesi community", one officer expressed.[13] Such behaviour of regional parties is creating obstacles to improve security in Madhes. The source of the problem is the failure of political parties, especially the regional parties to differentiate the crime and political acts, accepting criminalisation of politics and politicisation of crimes as their culture. Hence, unless politics of opportunism prevails against principles of democratic values and norms, neither SSS nor determination of the security forces to curb the crimes work effectively.

Only the strict implementation of the SSS cannot control crimes in Terai-Madhes unless regional parties and their leaders do not commit to ensure security. Vast majority of armed groups do not have political characters. Periodic convention, election of leaders, stated aims and objectives, formalisation through recognition from authorised bodies such as Election Commission are some of the common characteristics of any political groups. If we too examine the armed groups existing in Nepal, most of them do not fall under political force. They are involved in spreading terror and criminal activities in the name of Madhesi liberation. But, if the regional parties try to continuously politicise the armed groups, peace and security will just be a far-cry giving more space to communal violence.[14]

Over-politicisation, irresponsible acts of armed groups, unrealistic demands (such as 'One Madhes, One Province' and right to secession) and use of violence to fulfil one's own demand show that the situation could further worsen in future. Renouncing violence, stopping criminalisation of politics and politicisation of crimes and uniting people from diverse ethnic and communal background will only stop Madhes from being a political battlefield and a perennial source of conflict.

During the field observation, some local people said that the feelings of communal hatred in them erupt when the leaders visit their districts. They also said that their societies remain peaceful to some extent than in election times because ethnic slogans have not been chanted these days as the leaders are busy in the capital city. They expressed that when the leaders come to districts, they always make aggressive and bitter speeches targeting hill-people. It subsequently fuels communalism and antagonism.[15]

Madhesi leaders are using federalism and constitution-making as tools to divert attention of Madhesi people from scrutinising their political performance, ignorance towards people while in power and struggle among themselves when they break down party to get power, positions and resources. Respondents of the focus group discussion explained that if people critically question the role of Madhesi leaders in addressing socio-economic problems faced by Madhesi people, Madhesi leaders will have no satisfactory answers. Hence, 'One Madhes, One Province', 'Pahadi Nationalism', 'Exploitation from Kathmandu' are some of the catchy phrases to divert the people's scrutiny against them. The current approach of Madhesi leaders to deal on socio-economic issues, what we call 'political opportunism', does not work. Instead, it serves as perennial source of insecurity, communal disharmony, mistrusts and hatred and pushes into the protracted conflict.

Table 25 Killing and abduction in 20 Madhes districts-2010

S.N.	Districts	Perpetrator in killing					Perpetrator in abduction				
		The state	Madhesi activists/ Armed groups	Uniden-tified	Maoist and others	Total	State	Madhesi activists/ Armed groups	Un iden-tified	Maoist and others	Total
1	Jhapa	-	-	-	18	18	-	-	1	-	1
2	Morang	-	-	1	14	15	-	-	-	2	2
3	Sunsari	-	-	-	10	10	-	-	1	-	1
4	Saptari	-	2	1	11	14	-	1	1	19	21
5	Siraha	-	1	2	11	14	-	1	1	15	17
6	Dhanusha	6	3	1	20	30	-	-	-	8	8
7	Mahottari	1	2	-	11	14	-	1	2	5	8
8	Sarlahi	3	2	-	9	14	-	-	3	7	10
9	Rautahat	6	1	-	16	23	-	-	1	6	7
10	Bara	1	6	1	16	24	-	1	1	1	3
11	Parsa	5	1	1	7	14	-	-	-	1	1
12	Chitwan	-	-	-	1	1	-	-	-	4	4
13	Nawalparasi	-	-	-	9	9	-	-	1	8	9
14	Rupandehi	2	1	2	10	15	-	-	-	4	4
15	Kapilbastu	-	2	-	8	10	-	-	-	3	3
16	Dang	-	1	-	6	7	-	-	1	-	1
17	Banke	3	4	1	9	17	-	3	-	14	17
18	Bardiya	3	2	-	4	9	-	-	-	1	1
19	Kailali	-	-	-	3	3	-	-	-	4	4
20	Kanchanpur	-	-	-	2	2	-	-	-	1	1
	Total	30	28	10	195	263		7	13	103	123

Source: Adapted by the authors on the basis of INSEC (2011)

The study of INSEC (2011) as described in Table 25 shows that abduction and killing is continued even after election to the CA. Achieving security must be a priority of political parties and their leaders as well. It is not only the responsibility of security forces. But why violence in Madhes does not stop, why political leaders fail to realise the need of restoring peace and security, why every criminal cases are politicised, protected and negotiated, who is benefiting and who are losing from such activities? One should try to seek answers of these critical questions. The answers go to the political culture introduced in Nepal after the CPA, compromising constitutional provisions, rule of law, democratic ideas and values for the vested political party and individual interest of political leaders at both national and regional levels. Some of the thousands of examples illustrate such a culture. Failure to recruit the chief and other commissioners in Commission for Investigation on Abuses of Authority because of the interest of major political parties to send their party supporters, dividing constitutional and other sensitive positions (such as governor of the central bank, Vice-President of National Planning Commission, Autorney General, members of Public Service Commission or Election Comission, etc.) among the political parties, impunity to criminals proved by courts simply because of being donor, supporter or member of a certain political party and the bureaucracy controlled by trade unions are instances to this. Hence, the problem of Madhes is not only limited geographically but also complicated because of the national politics and political manipulation and therefore new thinking, new approach and new political order is required to address the current crisis of Nepal.

End note

1. See OCHA Nepal Situation Overview, Issue No. 52, August 2009.
2. MPRF leader Upendra Yadav had blamed that the SSS was launched to suppress Madhesi people's voice. For detail see http://www.solidaritykhabar.com/index.php?option=com_content&view=article&id=5273:2009-09-25-04-32-42&catid=1:2009-02-12-10-59-43&Itemid=67 accessed on 25 September 2009.

3. Matrika Yadav had blamed that it was against the Janajati and Madhesi people; for details, see http://www.nayapatrika.com/newsportal/permalink/6492.htm accessed 15th march 2011.
4. For details, see http://www.himalkhabar.com/hkp/news.php?id=2536; the information was accessed on 2 August 2010.
5. This event is related to the MPRF's street protest in Janakpur against the killing of Nawal Yadav, an outfit activist, by security forces.
6. For details, see www.ekantipur.com/Nepal/news/news-detail.php?news_id=542; the information was accessed on 2 August 2010.
7. For details, see http://www.ekantipur.com/kantipur/news/news-detail.php?news_id=5291; the information was accessed on 2 August 2010.
8. For details, see http://www.himalkhabar.com/hkp/news.php?id=2536; the information was accessed on 2 August 2010.
9. See *Nepal Weekly*, "*Aatmasamarpanle Dandahinatalai Prasraya*", 21 January 2009.
10. Interviews taken with the people of Janakpur on 11 February 2010
11. Kantipur National Daily, *Madhes Bidrohako Teen Barsa*, 21 January 2010.
12. CA member Karima Begum herself had gone to police post to release Mohar Kumar Chaudhary, who was charged as the mastermind of shooting to a businessman Om Prakash Chachan. Congress leader Radhe Chandra Yadav had also frequently pressurised security forces to release the people arrested from his district Bara. For details, see *Nepal Weekly*, Arko Bhesma Aparadhi, 10 August 2008.
13. Chief of the Dantakali Brigade of APF Prahlad KC as quoted in *Nepal Weekly*, Aparadhilai Unmukti, 2 December 2007.
14. *Nepali Times*, State of confusion, 13 July 2007.
15. Based on the FGDs in Mahottari, Saptari and Dhanusha districts.

7

Interests of International Actors

The geo-political location of Nepal and the changing power relations in South Asia together with growing strategic interests of Europe and the US in the region, the country is becoming a centre of diplomatic attention and interest-guided engamgent. The changing Sino-Indian dynamics (economic, security and political ambitions and associated complications) is both opportunity and threat to Nepal. This country can be easily used or abused by any international power players given the internal volatility and nature of underdevelopment here. Further, internal change in power relation (end of the monarchy, rise of Maoists, expansion of ethnic radicalism, communalisation of politics and emergence of regional forces), failure of national parties to lead the country, politicisation of the state mechanism including bureaucracy, security and judiciary, dominance of non-governmental organisations which are mostly patronised by particular donor interests, massive influence of international non-governmental organisation, lack of responsible private sector, intra-party tensions, etc.) are giving conducive environment to strong international manipulation in Nepal. Hence, at this critical political crossroad for this country, many international actors directly and indirectly engaged to fulfil their interests. However, this chapter limits to discuss international interests over Nepal's Terai-Madhes politics. India, China and other international actors in Nepal in forms of embassies, aid agencies and international non-governmental organisations have their own priorities on Terai-Madhes. This chapter is basically divided into three folds: interest of India, interest of China and interest of other western actors on the Terai-Madhes issue. The following first fold describes Indian interest and resultant effects.

7.1 Indian interest

Unambiguously, the involvement of Indian government is considered vital in Nepalese politics, especially on the Terai-Madhes issue. It is also possible because Nepal and India share free border covering the wide three directions of Nepal. Indian interest on Madhes issues of Nepal is clearly seen from the series of events and responses from Indian government whenever Terai-Madhes becomes an issue in the politics in Nepal. Indian interest over this issue can be categorised into three forms. The first is the interest of general Indian people, the second is that of the different Indian arm sellers and smugglers and the Indian politicians, and the third is that of the Indian government.

People to people relation

Indian people of neighbouring states of North India and Madhesi people of Nepal are close in terms of their cultural, social and economic ties. They have relations of 'Beti Aur Bahu' (of daughter and daughter-in-law/marital relations) or 'Roti Aur Beti' (of breads what they eat and daughters whom they marry) with Nepali Madhesis so they always feel empathy for the Nepalese Madhesis. This relationship between North Indian and Madhesi people reflected in cultural, religious and economic oneness is historical and a symbolic of friendship between the two countries. People of both sides cross the border for work, social exchange and pilgrimage.

In terms of work, the respondents in this research said that Indians want to come to Nepal because of the local opportunities and lower competition in Nepal. Many Indian businesspeople and shopkeepers want to expand their businesses to Nepal because of the capital they command and the competitive capacity they have to initiate business in Terai-Madhes. Further, Nepali business sector wants to give work to Indian workers because they are not the part of notorious trade unionism in Nepal and by doing so the businesses need not bear losses because of the strikes, padlocking and other intensive labour disputes.

In specific to the Indian people's role in the uprising in Terai-Madhes, the local Madhesis do not hesitate to say that they helped in the uprising as they are relatives and ethnic brothers of Nepali Madhesis. So, Indian people's involvement with Madhesi people in different walks of life is taken as general and natural. It is said that their support (be it moral or physical) is just due to the social, economical and cultural ties.

Indian landlords and politicians

Most of the politicians and bureaucrats of India do not hesitate to express their moral support to Madhesis (ICG 2007). These Indian leaders' support to Madhesis is guided by three reasons: one is ethnic similarities, socio-economic and cultural ties; the second, due to their intimacy with politics in Nepal. And the third is their vested economic interests. They do not want to lose their hold in their constituency areas. If Nepalese Maoists got strong hold in the southern areas of Nepal, it may affect the politics in adjacent Indian constituencies. So, most of these Indian leaders are serious on the Nepalese Maoists' growing influence and particularly their connection with Indian Naxalites and Maoists. Referring to a special report by the Ministry of Home Affairs in Nepal, a Nepalese daily had revealed the Indian politicians' involvement in the conflict and violence in Terai-Madhes.[1] The special report had claimed that a senior politician from Bihar had given support and protection to Madhesi armed groups in Nepal. Some Indian leaders have also started arms and ammunition deals with Madhesi armed groups. These leaders are also blamed to have provided military trainings and financial support to the groups. Not only the politicians, but also many landlords in Indian cities are said to be directly and indirectly involved in Madhes uprising and the politics in its aftermath as they do not want to see Maoists' rule in their adjacent districts which encourages Indian Maoist too (ICG 2007). The presence of the non-Maoist political force in Nepal's Terai-Madhes keeps their political carrier and status less threatened. Mathema (2011) and ICG (2007) also assume that the Gaur Carnage[2] is one of the results of these Nepalese as well as Indian landlords' and elites' response against the Maoists. Politically protected criminals are using open border to fulfil their interest and elites of both sides are instrumental in doing so. Nepal's Terai is also becoming a haven for criminals of Bihar once the Bihar government imposed strict rule of law that forced the criminals to leave Bihar.

Central government of India

India has been always active in the politics in Nepal directly or indirectly for several reasons. The reasons behind the interest of India over Madhesi issues can be described as follows:

a. Maintaining influence

India is using Terai-Madhes as a political tool to maintain its influence in Nepal. In the post-CPA times, the role of conventional allies of India changed and UCPN (M) emerged as a new force with which India always became cautious, worried and therefore dealt accordingly. This is the major framework of Indian engagement in Terai-Madhes after the CPA and election to the CA. The rise of Maoist force in Nepal and the suspicion from India that Nepalese Maoists could have strong tie with Indian Maoists had turned India more alert on Nepal. Indian fear rose higher after Nepalese Maoists bagged overwhelming votes in the elections to the CA in 2008. Thus, India sees it essential to strengthen Terai-Madhesi force to control over the southern plain in Indian favour. UCPN (M)'s anti-Indian rhetoric has further strengthened the Indian engagement in Terai-Madhes.

Terai-Madhes card is diplomatically important for India in different ways. First, Nepalese Maoists' inclination towards China, and the second, Nepalese Maoists' possible support to Indian Maoists and Naxalites who have become serious threat to internal security of India. The third reason is maintaining the loyalty of Terai-Madhesis towards India which was developed for a long time and which could work as butter at the time of expanded interest of China over Nepal and Terai-Madhes. Landlocked by India in three directions, it becomes hard for Nepal favourably negotiate in every issue with India. It is because India can geographically and socio-economically influence Nepal given the latter's long run dependence on India. Hence, Nepal's nearly total reliance with India (particularly transit and transport connection) and cultural proximity of North India and Terai-Madhes of Nepal are used by India as an opportunity for positional bargaining and strengthening the political forces in Terai-Madhes. Reason behind it is that India is successful to keep Terai-Madhes and regional parties under its influence. National parties are weak and their positions on certain issues such as citizenship certificate were always weakened by India that they had to compromise on every issues.

Nepali Maoists' behaviour against India and developing ties with China had been a nuisance for India. While leading the government, the Maoists were more inclined towards China than towards India. In the time of the Maoist government in Nepal, the leaders and cadres did regular visits to China. When then Prime Minister Pushpa Kamal Dahal as head of the government visited China first (to attend the openining ceremony of the Olympic game), India showed its dismay and then the Prime Minister had to say that it was an unofficial visit and he would do first official visit to India. India must have felt that it had brokered the peace deal as the Twelve-Point Understanding but the outcome then had been against Indian interests. It also must have been uncomfortable for India to see military trips of the Maoist ex-combatants visiting the northern neighbour. Besides, there was high frequency of visits of Chinese diplomats and security officials in Nepal. India took these all as an unusual interference and growing Chinese interest in Nepal. Further, the controversial audio tape scandal of (reportedly) Maoist leader Krishna Bahadur Mahara came into the media. It was a deal with a (reportedly) Chinese person asking for huge financial support to change the government in Nepal. It might have widened the suspicion of India. These activities of Nepalese Maoists fuelled the views of India which used to see Nepalese Maoists as close to China.[3] Different political leaders including Maoist supremo Prachanda had frequently expressed anti-Indian rage over the exploitation and unequal treatment from India. The Indian perception of growing anti-Indian feeling in Nepal and UCPN (M)'s role here is also a reason for India to aggressively engage in Nepal. Indian Ambassador to Nepal in 2010 had himself accepted that the anti-Indianism is growing in Nepal. Further, UCPN (M) affiliated trade unions are creating enormous problems to Indian companies in Nepal. Indian side has perceived it not only as a political but also a commercial threat for Indian business companies in Nepal.[4] But in all these activities, the role of other national parties is invisible. This may have warned India further. Hence, developing active political force countering anti-Indian interests and promoting Indian interest in Nepal is a strategy of India where Madhesi regional parties are used.

With growing economic might, China is also seeking wider political role in South Asia and Nepal. Frequent visit of Chinese envoys, their increasing influence over Nepalese issues and public assertions warning about China's readiness to respond to political destabilisation in Nepal has been a nuisance for India.[5] New Delhi has viewed increasing Chinese influence on India's neighbouring countries as an act to 'encircle' India (Nayak 2011).

With its assistance, India had hoped Nepalese Maoists to inspire Indian Maoists to come into peace process. But it turned the other way round. Worsening the situation, Nepalese Maoists, as India believes, are morally supported the insurgency of Indian Maoists. Nepalese Maoist leaders themselves accept their moral support to the Indian Maoists.[6] India has even claimed that the

Indian Maoists are getting military trainings in Nepalese Maoist cantonments.[7] Relation between Nepalese Maoists and India had once gone so worse that Nepalese Maoists showed black flags and misbehaved (by pelting stones) Indian Ambassador to Nepal across the country time and again.[8] One of the Maoist cadres had thrown his shoe to the Ambassador, Rakesh Sood, alleging him of interfering in Nepalese politics frequently.[9] It is also said that Indian ambassador had taken steps to Balkanise Nepal. That is why he had expressed his concerns on Madhesi grievances' in a way that organise Madhesis politically. Nayak (2011) adds that it later helped weaken Maoists and created a buffer between Maoists of the two countries in Terai-Madhes. Hence, India does not just turn deaf ear to the growing influence of Maoist over Nepal. It has developed strong hold over Madhesi issues and Madhesi parties throughout the time that help them play diplomatically with any political forces in Nepal. Aggressive direct Indian aids to construct schools, hospitals, trails and temples became more prominent to reach Indian influence at local level. Further, then Indian Ambassador to Nepal, Rakesh Sood, had started behaving like Nepalese politicians. He went to villages and districts and gave political speeches warning that if people would talk against India, he would stop aid and so on.

To deal with Nepalese issues, India has taken Terai-Madhesi parties as the strong force to be utilised against the Establishment. In different times, Indian leaders and diplomats come to Nepal and meet Madhesi leaders in Indian Embassy. Then Ambassador of India to Nepal, Rakesh Sood, has also urged to the Government of Nepal to settle the problem in Madhes peacefully, which drew him under controversy for going beyond the diplomatic ethics. Amidst, some Madhesi politicians themselves accept that they have been utilised by Indian interest (ICG 2007). Some Madhesi leaders also request for Indian support to 'fight against' the Kathmandu-centred government.

If politicians from Terai-Madhes do not fulfil the Indian expectation, India for sure will also play with them to keep them under its control. This is reflected in the frequent split of Terai-

Madhesi parties in Nepal. The split of MPRF is taken as an Indian step.[10] The MPRF-Nepal led by Upendra Yadav has been viewed as leftist since it made coalition government with the Maoists. Nayak (2011) writes that the formation of Terai Madhes Democratic Party (TMDP) was the conspiracy of India against the MPRF. Terai-Madhesi parties have been the arithmetic tool for Indian forces to form or topple down governments in Nepal. By this, India can have nuclear presence in every government thereby fulfilling Indian interest in Nepal.

b. Indian internal security

Nepal is a very sensitive neighbour to India due to its geo-political situation. Berkeley (1971 as cited in Gaige 2009) has written that India had been looking at Nepal as 'a dagger aimed at the heartland of the northern India'. India is always suspicious about the security threats from Nepalese territory. The officials from this country have been always highlighting the possibility of anti-Indian elements using Nepalese land to create insecurity in India.[11] Nayak (2011) claims that due to the weak security system in Nepal, by taking benefit of open border, Pakistan Directorate of Inter Services Intelligence (ISI) and Lashkar-e-Toiba (LeT) have increased its anti-Indian activities from the jungles along India-Nepal border, these organisations also sponsored lots of Madarassas in the border area. To some extent, India's security vulnerability in Himalaya is China's strength. So, the US and its other 'liberal' allies want to guarantee that India's northern defence system is adequate (Gaige 2009) to counter China. Arms smuggling, Pakistani criminals' engagement in fake Indian currency cases and Nepal becoming a transit point for illegal trade of narcotics, drugs and other products also became Indian security concern. Hence, Indian security intelligence is very active in Nepal. The details of how Indian intelligence is active in Nepal are illustrated by Shah (2010) and Adhikari (2009). They reveal a pathetic scenario on to what extent is Indian intelligence active in Nepal and why they are active.

India perceives Terai-Madhes as the most prone region in Nepal to be influenced by anti-Indian elements. Particularly, it fears whether this region provides space to both China and Pakistan to support anti-Indian elements with the help of arms smuggling, fake currency and drug trafficking by terrorist outfits (Nayak 2011). That is why India is always alert on what happens in this bordering region. Many of the security concerns raised by India are genuine and need immediate actions from the Government of Nepal as it could create devastating effects if we do not take actions.

7.2 Chinese interest

China is no more silent nowadays in the politics of South Asia as it is ambitiously rising to be a global powerhouse. China and India, two giants and powerful neighbours of Nepal, are in competition to be global economic powers. There had been military clashes between these countries in late 1950s and early 1960s. So, one of the grave concerns for both of them is the increasing influence of the other country. India perceives China as a big threat (Gaige 2009) if the latter is active in Nepal. Indian side views Chinese activities in the South Asian countries as the diplomacy to strategically encircle India (Nayak 2011).[12] When New Delhi's relation with Dhaka was not so smooth, Beijing and Dhaka got along very well. There was already border clash between Bangladesh and India. China has a good relation with Sri Lanka; so, Beijing gives arms to Colombo to fight against Liberation Tiger of Tamil Eelam (LTTE) and develop port in the south. Similarly, growing Sino-Pakistani relation has also been a source of nuisance to India.[13] China is strongly supporting military of Pakistan in addition to other economic cooperation, for which India has both worries and concerns. Hence, Sino-Indian relation is not limited to economic opportunities, as many analysts argue, it is very strongly entangled in the security concerns in South Asia. Once China expanded its engagement in Terai-Madhes, it has been another concern for India.

The most serious Indo-Nepalese dispute had occurred once Nepal allowed China to construct the Lhasa-Kathmandu road after the Sino-Indian conflict in 1962. India considered this move as Nepal's acquiescence to China's overall military strategy in South Asia. Arguing this Dash (1996) puts forth that Indo-Nepal relations remained at low ebb during 1960s and the 1970s. During the rule of the monarch, stable collaboration of China in Nepal was with palace, not with the communists and liberal parties. But after the king's exit from the palace, China was seeking a strong political ally in Nepal. The Maoists' overwhelming victory in the election to the CA in 2008 gave political space for the China to be nearer to Nepalese Maoists. Further, anti-Indian position of UCPN (M) also helped them be close to China. Though China has not still fully relied on UCPN (M) as its stable ally, the party seems to be under Chinese probation. In this opportunity, which coincided with the growing economic might of China in the world, Beijing has begun to strengthen its political connection with Nepal.

Now Beijing has increased its development assistance along with diplomatic concerns in Nepal. Chinese firms are enlarging investments in infrastructure projects in Nepal day by day. Chinese support to Armed Police Force of Nepal also shows strategic interest of this northern neighbour. China is now said to have the third highest Foreign Direct Investment (FDI) in Nepal after India and the US.[14] Indian diplomats time and again express dissent over the increasing northern influence in Nepal. They opine that China has been taking much greater interest in Nepal. They perceive this as a Chinese act to become more visible and assertive in affecting India's interests in Nepal.[15]

Unlike India which used diplomacy and various forms of aids to influence Nepal (Gaige 2009), China had not had such covert influence until the entrance of Maoists in Nepalese mainstream politics and the end of monarchy.[16] It mainly gives attention to Nepal because it is aware that India with other western forces will use Nepalese territory to strengthen Tibetan freedom movement and play against the growing Chinese power. After the peace agreement in 2006, many US diplomats visiting Nepal do vehemently raise the issue of Tibet with Nepalese government.

Even some US Senators and politicians have threatened that they will stop aid to Nepal if it does not show liberal approach towards the activities of Tibetan refugees and supporters in Nepal. China has been serious on such high concerns from American, Indian and other western countries on Tibet issue. The Chinese government perceives that this influence can fuel the Free Tibet Movement from Nepalese soil.[17] China has raised concern time and again on the anti-Chinese role of Tibetan refugees. Further, China is suspicious that nearly 20,000 Tibetan refugees residing in Nepal can be used as rebels against it. With every Chinese delegate, Nepal has been assuring that it would not allow anti-China activities and Nepal is fully committed to 'One China' policy. But China seems to have recently taken another approach to deal with India in this issue by giving higher attention to the Terai-Madhes that threatens India. This is why there are increasing involvement of China in the Indo-Nepal in forms of a number of China Study Centres across the country and massive investment in the Terai region. As a tit-for-tat response, India has invested in numerous projects in the Sino-Nepal border areas.

China has also made efforts to establish relation with Terai-Madhes political parties too. Nayak (2011) claims that after Upendra Yadav stopped getting support from India once he aligned the Maoists, his faction of MPRF got support from China. A high level of Chinese delegation was present on the general convention of MPRF-Nepal in early 2009. Further, China has boosted its presence in Southern part of Nepal. Recently, 33 China Study Centres have been established in the Nepalese southern districts, which are close to Indian border (Cheah 2008). China has recently announced an investment worth three billion US dollar to build Lumbini as a World Peace City in honour to the Lord Buddha. This investment has been viewed as one of the strategic steps of China in the Indo-Nepal border.[18]

China and India might have their own interest but Nepal have to find its own interest among theirs. In the changed scenario, Nepal need to reshape its foreign policy, it has to make balanced relation between the both equally important neighbours. Weak and less-sighted foreign policy can worsen the relation among the three countries, which will be unsupportive for the peace in the whole Asian region. However, Nepal's foreign policy is not able to cope up with the strategic challenges faced by Nepal.

7.3 Western interests

Now, Madhes has been an interest for not merely India and China. There is a growing interest from the US and European countries in this issue. Their investments in Madhesi NGOs and dealing with Madhesi leaders highlight their focus to Terai-Madhes issues. It rose higher especially after the CPA, during the Terai-Madhes revolt and during the times of elections to the CA. Different reports (Rawal 2011a and 2011b) claim that aid agencies are continuously focusing on Terai-Madhes issues with huge flow of money after 2008. Financial support from aid agencies to ethnic organisations to raise their issues during the time of elections triggered severe criticism because of the timing of the aid-flow. Arguments say that international agencies should not have tried to affect elections with their immediate flow of financial resources. Ethically, they should be neutral and this is more required in times of democratic elections. However, their activities were severely criticised. Even in Nepalese political circle, media and analysts expressed severe dismay on the ambition of the then UNMIN Head to link Madhes issue into CPA and engage in economic rights issues. Indeed, they all were totally out of the UNMIN mandate. Some political leaders publicly opposed such interests of UNMIN. It is still widely believed that one of the fuelling factors of Madhes revolt was the radicalisation of people's sentiment by international actors in the name of 'rights' and 'empowerment'.

International actors have been heavily supporting Madhesi actors. These supports include intellectual as well as financial assistance to the caucus of Terai-Madhesi law-makers. Danish, American, Swiss, British, Finnish and Canadian aid agencies have been very active in the past few years. But their approach to address the issue is not uncontroversial. Lack of transparency in aid agencies and weakening the state at the time of transition by funding parallel structures (NGOs) in uncoordinated way and channelling huge budget have further aggravated the problem instead of providing solutions.

Some of the projects funded by major donors such as the Alternative Dispute Resolution project named as Madhesi Community Mediation suffered criticism even from the judicial sector which hardly involves in such overtly verbal comments. Its main objective was to bring the belligerent parties in negotiation before reaching it to the police and judiciary. Rawal (2011b) argues it as a contradictory practice because the government itself has established Reconciliation Centre (Melmilap Kendra) in 79 courts. He terms it as a practice of parallel government encouraged by the aid agencies. Otherwise, such projects must be designed to the Reconciliation Centres of the court instead of working parallelly on the same issue. In addition, such agencies have been also supporting Armed Police Force and other security agencies active in Terai-Madhes.

Understandably, in a psychologically divided country, some political, social and NGO leaders from Terai-Madhes have been defending such parallel project supports. They argue that the programmes by international agencies in Terai-Madhes focus on empowering the local people. Of course, such assistance may have good intention to bring the marginalised people into the front; but such an unplanned, a controversial and a disintegrated approach of development and flow of resources may cost high in sensitive issues such as identity and ethnicity.

End note

1. *Kantipur National Daily*, Ek Saya Nau Samuhako Chirphar, 1 August 2009.
2. Gaur Carnage took place on 21 March 2007 where 28 people were mercilessly killed in the encounter between the cadres of MPRF and UCPN (Maoist).
3. *Nepali Times*, Two Dajus, 29 August 2008.

4. *The Times of India*, Nepal Maoists' support for Indian comrades worries govt, 1 July 2010.
5. *Nepali Times*, Two Dajus, 29 August 2008.
6. *Deccan Herald*, Nepali Maoists confirm support to Indian Naxals, 3 November 2010
7. *Deccan Herald*, Maoist arms training row refuses to die down in Nepal, 20 November 2010
8. Even one of the Maoist senior leader such as polit-bureau member was involved in doing so. See: *Republica*, Maoists show Sood black flags, 1 March 2011
9. *The Kathmandu Post*, Case filed against Sood 'shoe-thrower', 16 December 2010
10. *Nepali Times*, Venting it out in Varanasi, 3 October 2008.
11. *The Himalayan Times*, India raises security concerns with MPs, 26 November 2010
12. For more discussion, see *Nepali Times*, Two Dajus, 29 August 2008.
13. Pranab Dhal Samanta, 'The India factor' in *Nepali Times*, 18 February 2011.
14. See interview with K.V. Rajan in Utpal Parashar's write-up in *Hindustan Times*, India losing little great game, 4 September 2010.
15. Ibid.
16. For details, see *The Himalayan Times*, Tibetan poll bid foiled, 21 March 2011
17. For details, see *The Himalayan Times*, China concerned about statute delay, 25 March 2011
18. For details, see *Times of India*, Maoists signed controversial Buddha deal, says Chinese envoy, 9 August 2011.

8

CONCLUSIONS

There are miles to go in the long-run process of addressing to the genuine issues of Terai-Madhes and the ethnic division implanted since 2007 Terai revolt. Some issues could be instantly solved; some needs proper planning, process and institutionalisation to realise the change. In the changed politics, people have confusions over some new issues such as federalisation, marking of the federal boundaries, creating national symbols and recognising identity. Further, these issues are blatantly politicised and conscious efforts have been made to confuse people by opposing the open, constructive debate on exploring major possible options on the models of federalism. Minority groups are expressing fears that they may be further suppressed in the proposed federalisation if it is based on caste and ethnicity. Indigenous Tharus and other minority groups are strongly opposing the demand of 'One Madhes, One Province' by Madhesi elites. Hence, the fear of future insecurity is fuelling communalism. If political parties, government and Madhesi elites do not play concrete roles in addressing this situation and assuring every group of their rights, the situation is likely to spread heavy communal hatred among different caste groups in Terai-Madhes. It will be costly even for those who wish to get political benefits from such communal tensions.

It is not a good way to enforce inclusion with the help of revenge, retaliation and promotion of communal tension. It is possible from forward thinking, co-existence, social harmony and concerted action. For Terai-Madhes to be inclusive, prosperous and stable, whole Nepal has to be the same. Hence, the current thinking, behaviour and practices of Madhesi leaders as well as the leaders of other political parties and civil society need strategic shift in their behaviour and attitude.

The trend of forming and supporting armed groups and raising the issues of ethnic state has spread fear to minority groups in Terai-Madhes. People are feeling insecure due to heavy militarisation of youths and their criminal activities targeting to particular communities. Armed groups are mushrooming and are incited by vested interests to raise personal agenda. This has also been fostering anarchy and insecurity. It has fuelled communal hostility. A different approach to tackle with the armed groups as majority of them has criminal attributes with no political characteristics.

A much-needed assistance is from India in controlling trans-border crimes. This will help India too in combating insecurity there. If Terai-Madhes continues to be played by national and international actors in their respective interest; the cost is going to be very high for the neighbouring countries too. So, both national and regional parties should take initiative to restore peace and harmony in Terai-Madhes taking into mind that this region is sensitive not only to Nepal and neighbouring countries, but also to the whole Asian region. Yes, ethnicity and ethnic rights should be properly respected and recognised; but such things should not be a political ploy to use opportunistically. The trend of misusing caste, class and ethnic system would certainly cost the society an irreparable loss. We should learn from former Yugoslavia, former Soviet Union, North-East India, Ethiopia and many other countries who are now paying price of ethnic politicisation.

While addressing to the issues of Terai-Madhes, the most important is to address the issues of the minority Terai-Madhesi groups. It is because their voice is not only politically poorly represented but also diverted by the powerful elites of Terai-Madhes for their vested interests. The elitist nature of Terai-Madhes politics has not represented all the pains and pathos of the southern demography of the country.

During the autocratic Panchayat regime, Madhesi people were largely deprived in terms of identity such as language, inclusion, autonomy and civil rights. Panchayat system used the Madhesi elites and landlords to suppress the poor, marginalised and landless people of Madhes. The legacy of this system still exists especially in those elites, who are turned as Madhesi leaders now. The post-1990 democratic governments have worked a lot to address the genuine issues of Madhes. However, the Mahdesi elites are not ready to change themselves. The prominent example is the resistance to land reform.

Constantly creating artificial divide between Madhesi and Pahadi community residing together in harmony for centuries, Madhesi elite leaders are not even ready to implement land reform. The most skewed land distribution exists in Madhes. Exploitation and marginalisation is far more rampant here but the regional leaders, who are frequently in key power, are not ready to address to these problems. Thus, only providing blanket reservation and practising lump sum positive discrimination in cluster under 'Madhesi' tag will not work well as there are a number of disadvantaged groups inside Terai-Madhes. Such groups' concern are neither accepted by Madhesi elites nor internalised. Rather, they are diffused under the rubric of 'One Madhes, One Province'. Their level of deprivation is severe on the basis of caste, class and cultural practices and the sources of such deprivation is the exploitative nature of power relation between marginalised/ excluded people and elites in this region.

The relative ignorance towards Terai-Madhesi people by the ruling elite mainly before 1990's political change is used by Madhesi political leaders as opportunities for political bargaining or revenge. It is also to cover their inaction for the Terai-Madhesi people during their stay in power. Similarly, some 'analysts', Madhesi civil society leaders and NGO activists have tactfully used Madhes issue as an opportunity to obtain resources and establish relations with international power centres and the media. The post-CPA role of some of such groups is largely contributing to communal tension and ethnic divide instead of promoting co-existence and harmony.

Terai-Madhes in the past was struggling on five major concerns: language, identity, autonomy, inclusion and representation. However, since the signing of CPA in 2006, many of these concerns are addressed by the Interim Constitution and implementation process is in progress. At present, Terai-Madhesi people are in key power positions such as President, Vice-president, Deputy Prime Minister and half of the ministers in the UCPN (M)-led government by Dr Baburam Bhattarai. They are properly represented in the CA. The inclusion issue is incorporated in the Acts and regulations. In the post-CA election times, Madhesi leaders are well-represented in the cabinet and influential in decision-making. However, they have not yet properly worked for Madhesis while being in power. Instead, they are fighting to grab power and for that they even split own parties. Madhesi parties are split into a number of factions after the election to the CA. They have reversed the established principle of 'united we win' and laid the new principle of 'divided we grab power'. After the observation of the behaviour of Madhesi parties and their leaders during the past six years, one can safely conclude that they are working to grab the state power and resources than working to address the pertinent issues of Terai-Madhes.

The conflict in Terai-Madhes has displaced numerous hill-origin people. Such displacement will generate hatred between the communities for generations. The Hutu and Tutsi ethnic tension in Rwanda has offered a very costly lesson to this world and Nepal must learn from and internalise this. It needs sense of security and feeling of the protection from impunity in people to live dignified life within the country. Along with this, reorienting misled youths and demilitarising them is essential in the case of growing militarisation of young minds in the Terai region. Their needs such as opportunity to education and employment as well as dignified rehabilitation and socio-political reconciliation are not yet taken care of. Constructive role of Madhesi leaders and elite is crucial in achieving this.

The most importantly, political leaders and their public speeches represent their intellect, wisdom and people's voice. They are sensitive factors for a conciliatory future. Therefore, the leaders must not deliver controversial speeches radicalising one community against others. Sovereignty and independence is always precious, so is the integrity of the country. Solutions should be sought in unity, not in division.

One can observe from Nepalese political events that the national parties have been trying to appease Terai-Madhesi parties in the time of every new government formation. The latter are also more engaged on bargaining for the political power that they gain, not what the Terai-Madhesis get. The state mechanisms and the government should more be attentive to the genuine issues of grass-root Terai-Madhesis to solve the problem. The upcoming Constitution, if promulgated by consensus, or at least the highest level of political understanding among the mainstream political forces, could be a good beginning to empower the marginalised people of Nepal. This will also pave a way for Terai-Madhesis to live dignified life as Nepalese citizens.

The writings and analysis of scholars and journalists like Tula Narayan Shah, Prasant Jha, CK Lal, Chandra Kishore, Kanak Dixit, Yubaraj Ghimire, Saroj Raj Adhikari and many others and the expressions of political activists and leaders like Mahanta Thakur, Rajendra Mahato, Upendra Yadhav, Keshav Mainali, Jetendra Dev, Jaya Prakash Gupta, Anil Jha, Bimelendra Nidhi, Ram Chandra Jha, and others and the writings in the weekly magazine 'Voice of Madhes' published by Madhes Media House as well as analysis of international conflict and peace research organisations like PRIO (Miklian, 2009) and ICG and the reports of human rights organisations like INSEC (2007-2011) indicate that the Terai-Madhes in a critical cross-road. In this context, a collective thinking and concerted action from all sectors of society (academia and researchers, business people, journalists, activist groups; and all political parties (regional or national) is urgently needed to address the genuine concerns of Terai-Madhes (social exclusion and marginalisation of powerless, elite capture of resrources, power and positons, politiciasation of security, militerisation of youth, expansion of communal hatred and revenges etc. participation of excluded in political decision making, establishing rule of law and promoting, socio-cultural, economic and political rights of people of terai-madhes).

References

Adhikari J, Dhungana H, Dev O. (2006). Terai ko Banbyabasthan. In: B. Thapa, and M. Mainali, *Madhes Samasya ra Sambhawana* (pp. 55-83). Lalitpur: Social Science Baha.

Adhikari Sarojraj. (2009). *Jasusiko Jalo*. Kathmandu: Pairavi Book House.

Ahmad Z. (2003). The Bihari Muslims of Bangladesh in a State of Statelessness. In P. Chari, M. Joseph, and S. Chandaran, *Missing Boundaries, Refugees, Migrants, Stateless and Internally Displaced Persons in South Asia* (pp. 173-180). New Delhi: Manohar Publishers and Distributers.

Asian Center for Human Right. (2009). *Madhes: Challenge and Opportunities for a Stable Nepal.* Asian Center for Human Right.

Bauböck R. (2002). *How Migration Transforms Citizenship:International, Multinational and Transnational Perspectives.* IWE.

Bhattachan KB. (2000). Possible Ethnic Revolution or Insurgency in a Predatory Unitary Hindu State, Nepal. In D. K. Kumar, *In Domestic Conflict and Crisis of Governability in Nepal* (pp. 154-55). Kathmandu: Center for Nepal and Asian Studies.

Bhattachan KB. (2008). *Minorities and Indigenous People of Nepal.* Kathmandu: National Coalition Against Racial Discrimination (NCARD).

Biswakarma H. (2008). Nijamati Sewa maa Samabesikaran. In A. Ajit, *Samabesikaran Rajnitik Dal, Rajya ra Media* (pp. 41-69). Kathmandu: Martine Chautari.

Burkert C. (1997). Defining Maithali Identity: Who is in Charge? In D. N. Gellener, *Nationalism and Ethnicity in a Hindu Kingdom:The Politics of Culture in Contemporary Nepal* (pp. 241-274). Amsterdam: Harwood Academic Publishers.

CBS [Central Bureau of Statistics]. (2001). *Population Census 2001 of Nepal.* Kathmandu: National Planning Commission, CBS, HMG.

CBS [Central Bureau of Statistics]. (2003). *Population Monograph of Nepal, VOl I.* Kathmandu: CBS.

CBS [Central Bureau of Statistics]. (2009). *Statistical Year Book of Nepal 2009.* Kathmandu: CBS.

Chaudhary, D. (2008). *Nepalko Madhesi Samaj (Madhesi Society in Nepal).* Kathmandu: Ratna Pustak Bhandar.

Chaudhary M. (2007). *Nepalko Terai tatha Yaska Bhumiputraharu.* Kathmandu: Shanti Chaudhary.

Cheah F. (2008). Inclusive Democracy for Madheshis: The Quest for Identity, Rights and Representation. Institute of South Asian Studies (ISAS).

Dahal D. (1996). Madhesiya Pahadiya Antar Sambandha (Madheshi Pahadi Interrelationship). Kathmandu: Himal.

Dash KC. (1996). The Political Economy of Regional Cooperation in South Asia. *Pacific Affairs*, 69(2).

EC [Election Commission]. (1999). *Pratinidhisabha Sadasya Niwarchan 1999 (2056).* Kathmandu: Election Commission.

EC [Election Commission]. (2008). *Sambidhan Sabha Sadsya Niwarchan, 2064 Niwarchan Parinam Pustika.* Kathmandu: Election Commission.

Farzana KF. (2008). The Neglected Stateless Bihari Community in Bangladesh: Victims of Political and Diplomatic Onslaught. *Journal of Humanities and Social Science,* Volume 2, Issue 1 .

Financial Controller General Office (2007). *Government of Nepal Consolidated Financial Statements Fiscal Year 2005/2006.* Kathmandu: Government of Nepal.

Financial Controller General Office. (2008). *Government of Nepal Consolidated Financial Statements Fiscal Year 2006/2007.* Kathmandu: Government of Nepal.

Gaige FH. (2009, 1st edition 1975). *Regionalism and National Unity in Nepal.* Kathmandu: Himal Books.

Gautam B. (2008). *Madhes Bidhroha ko Naalibeli.* Kathmandu: Martin Chautari.

Gellener DN. (2007, May 19). *Caste, Ethnicity and Inequality in Nepal.* Economic and Political Weekly .

Gellener D, Pfaff-Czarnecka J, Whelpton J. (1997). *Nationalism and Ethnicity in a Hindu Kingdom.* The Netherlands: Harwood Academic Publishers.

Gellner DN. (2005). *Ethnic Rights and Politics in Nepal.* Himalayan Journal of Sociology and Anthropology , 1-17.

Guneratne A. (2009). Introduction . In FH. Gaige, *Regionalism and Nationality Unity in Nepal*. Lalitpur: Himal Books, pp. XVI-XXVII.

Gupta JP. (2006). *Srilanka ko Tamil: Bibhed Bhitra Ko Bidhroha.* Kathmandu: Madhesi Manawa Adhikar Samranchan Kendra.

Gupta JP. (2010). *Madhes Pradhes ko Prastawana (Proposal for Madhes Region).* Kathmandu: Madhesi Manawa Adhikar Samranchan Kendra.

Gurung H. (2001). *Nepal: Social Demography and Expressions.* Kathmandu: New Era.

Gurung H. (2005). *Nepal Regional Strategy for Development.* Asian Development Bank.

Gurung H. (2010). *Bishaya Bibidh* . Kathmandu : Ratna Pustak Bhandar.

Gurung H. (1989). Regional Patterns of Migration in Nepal. *Papers of the east west population institute, 0732-0531; no 113.* Hawaii: Library of Congress Cataloging in Publication Data.

Hachhethu K. (2007). *Nepali Nationalisms and Restructuring the Nepali State.* Kathmandu: Center for Nepal and Asian Studies Center.

Hangen S. (2007). Creating a "New Nepal": The Ethnic Dimension. *Policy Studies 34* .

Hangen S. (2010). *The Rise of Ethnic Politics in Nepal.* New Delhi: Routledge.

Housden O. (2009). *Nepal: A Failing State or A State in Transition.* New Delhi: Institute of Peace and Conflict Studies.

Human Right Watch. (2003). *Trapped by Inequality: Bhutanese Refugee Women in Nepal.* Human Right Watch Vol 15. No. 8 (C).

Human Rigths Law Network. (2007). *Report of Refugee Populations in India.* Human Rigths Law Network.

Hyome K. (2006). Madhesipratiko Bived ra Samanta Aandolan. In B. Thapa, and M. Mainali, *Madhes: Samasya ra Sambhawana* (pp. 112-124). Lalitpur: Social Science Baha.

ICG [International Crisis Group] . (2003). *Nepal Backgrounder:Ceasefire – Soft Landing or Strategic Pause?* Kathmandu/ Brussels: ICG.

ICG [International Crisis Group]. (2007). *Nepal's Troubled Tarai Region.* Kathmandu/Brussels: ICG.

ICG [International Crisis Group]. (2011). *Nepal: Identity Politics and Federalism.* Kathmandu/ Brussels: ICG.

ICIMOD. (2003). *Districts of Nepal Indicators of Development Update* . Kathmandu: ICIMOD.

Interdisciplinary Analysts, Nepal Madhes Foundation, Small Arms Survey and Safer World. (2011). *Armed Violence in the Terai.* Kathmandu: IDA, NMF, SAS and Safer World.

INSEC. (2007). *Nepal Human Rights Year Book 2007.* Kathmandu: INSEC.

INSEC. (2008). *Nepal, Human Rights Year Book 2008.* Kathmandu: INSEC.

INSEC. (2009). *Nepal Human Rights Year Book 2009.* Kathmandu: INSEC.

INSEC. (2010). *Nepal, Human Rights Year Book 2010.* Kathmandu: INSEC.

INSEC. (2011). *Nepal Human Rights Year Book 2011.* Kathmandu: INSEC.

Jha HB. (1993). *The Terai Community and National Integration in Nepal.* Kathmandu: Center for Economic and Technical Studies (CETS).

Jha HB. (2010). *The Economy of Terai Region of Nepal: Prospects for Its Sustainable Development.* Lalitpur: Centre for Economic and Technical Studies (CETS).

Kansakar VB. (2003). International Migration and Citizenship in Nepal. In CBS, *Population Monograph of Nepal Vol II* (pp. 85-119). Kathmandu : CBS.

KC BK. (1998). *Trends, Patterns and Implications of Rural to Urban Migration in Nepal.* Kathmandu: Central Department of Population Studies, Tribhuvan University.

Lal CK. (2002). Cultural Flows Across a Blurred Boundry. In K. M. Dixit, and R. Shastri, *State of Nepal* (pp. 100-118). Kathmandu: Himal Books.

Malla UT. (2010). *Collaborative Approach to Madhes Conflict Resolution.* [Master's Thesis]. University of San Diego.

Middleton T, Schneiderman S. (2008, May 10). Reservations, Federalism, and Politics of Recognition in Nepal. *Economic and Political Weekly* .

Miklian J. (2009). *Nepal's Terai: Constructing an ethnic Conflict.* Oslo: International Peace Research Institute.

Nayak N. (2011). The Madhesi Movement in Nepal:Implication for India. *Strategic Analysis* , 35:4, 640-660.

Neupane G. (2000). *Nepal Ko Jatiya Prashna.* Kathmandu.

Neupane G. (2005). *Nepal ko Jatiya Prashna Samajik Banot ra sajhedariko Sambhawana.* Kathmandu.

Neyazi T. A. (2007). State, Citizenship and Religious Community: The Case of Indian Muslim Women. *Asian Journal of Political Science Vol. 15, No. 3,* , 303 - 318.

Nubin W. (2002). *Sri Lanka: current issues and historical background.* New York: NOVA.

Pathak B, Niraula C. (2007). *Madhes Violence: Identity Clash in Nepal.* Kathmandu: Conflict Study Center.

Pathak B, Uprety D. (2009). Terai-Madhes Searching for Identity Based Security. *Situation Update*, pp. 1-27. Kathmandu: Conflict Study Center.

Pathak B, Uprety D. (2010). *Pat Disarmament Demobilization and Reintegration and Security Sector Reform in Nepal: A Preliminary Sociological Observation. Situation Update 90, 7 March 2010.* Kathmandu: Conflict Study Center.

Paudel SB. (2010). Madhes Conflict and Changed Social Relationship: A Case Study of Bardibas VDC, Mahottari District [Master's Thesis], Kathmandu University.

Paudel SB, Ghimire A. (2010). Internally Displaced Persons. In NCCR and NIDS, *Nepal Migration Year Book 2009* (pp. 60-70). Kathmandu: NCCR North- South and NIDS.

Pradhan R, Shrestha A. (2005). *Ethnic And Caste Diversity: Implicaation for Development.* Asian Development Bank.

Rawal RB. 2011a. Madhesma Dollarko Varshaa, *Nepal Weekly*, 25 September 2011.

Rawal RB. 2011b. Jaatiyatalaai Maljal, *Nepal Weekly*, 25 December 2011.

Regmi MC. (1978). *A Studies in Nepali Economic History.* New Delhi: Manjushree Publishing House.

Satyal VR. (2003). *Population Dynamics of Muslims in Nepal, Number 25 and 26.* Kathmandu: Institute for Integrated Development Studies (IIDS).

Sen A. (2006). *Identity and Violence.* Great Britain : Allen lane.

Shah B. (2010). *Maile Dekheko Durbar.* Kathmandu: Yeti Publications.

Shah N, Roukema JS, Rajbhandari G. (2010). *The Controversy between Trails and Rural Roads:The Case of Nepal.* Kathmandu: The International Forum for Rural Transport and Development (IFRTD).

Shah G. (2006). *Socila Inclusion of Madhesi Community.* Kathmandu .

Shah G. (2008). *Peaceful Resolution of Ethnopolitical Movement in Nepal Madhesh.* Non Resident Madheshis.

Subedi BP. (2007). The Issue of Foreign Born Population in Nepal:A Short Essay in Honor of Dr. Harka Gurung. *The Himalayan Review 38 (2007) 23-34.*

Thapa N. (2009). *Country Profile of Excluded Groups in Nepal* (Draft). UN ESCAP.

UNDP [United Nations Development Programme] (1998). *Nepal Human Development Report 1998.* Kathmandu: Nepal South Asia Centre.

UNDP [United Nations Development Programme]. (2004). *Nepal, Human Development Report 2004.* Kathmandu: UNDP.

UNDP[United Nations Development Programme]. (2009). *Nepal Human Development Report 2009.* Kathmandu: UNDP.

Upreti B.C. (2006). Nagarikita ko Rajniti (Politics of Citizenship). In B. Thapa, and M. Mainali, *Madhes Samasya ra Sambhawana (Madhes Probelms and Opputunity)* (pp. 99-111). Lalitpur: Social Science Baha.

Upreti BR. (2008). Land and Social Conflict. In B. R. Upreti, S. S. Raj, and B. Jagat, *Land Politics and Conflict in Nepal* (pp. 109-141). Kathmandu: NCCR North South.

Upreti BR. (2009). *Nepal from war to peace.* Kathmandu: NCCR-North South.

Whelpton J, Gellner ND, Pfaff- Czarnecka J. (2008). *New Nepal, New Ethnicities: Changes Since the mid -1990s', Preface in Nationalism and Ethnicity in Nepal.* Kathmandu: Vajra Books.

Wolff S. (2007). *Ethnic conflict: a global perspectives.* Oxford University press.

Yadav R. (2006a). Madheshi Hunda (Being Madheshi). In B. Thapa, and M. Mainali, *Madhesh: Samsya ra Sambhabana (Madhesh: Problems and Opportunity).* Kathmandu: Social Science Baha.

Yadav R. (2006b). *Madhesi: A Disvantaged Social Group.* Kathmandu: Jaghrit Nepal.

Yadav U. (2007). *Madhes aur Madhesi: Samasya aur Samadhan.* Kathmandu: Madhesi Janadhikar Forum.

Annexes

Annex 1: List of the Armed Groups Active in Nepal

1. Ajingar Axe
2. Akhil Terai Mukti Morcha
3. Akhil Terai Mukti Morcha (Goit)
4. Akhil Terai Mukti Morcha (Pratap)
5. Dinosaur
6. Defence Nepal of Trishul Sena
7. GFFAP Ranvir Sena Nepal
8. Gorkha Mukti Morcha
9. Hindu Rastra Nirman Sena
10. Hindu Sena
11. International Tigers
12. Janabad Ganatantrik Terai Mukti Morcha
13. Janabad Terai Mukti Morcha
14. Janakranti Mukti Moorcha
15. Janakranti Terai Mukti Morcha (Ranvir)
16. Janakranti Terai Mukti Morcha (Tufan)
17. Janakranti Terai Mukti Morcha (Himmat Group)

18. Janakranti Terai Mukti Morcha (Pawan)
19. Janashakti Krantikari Party
20. Janatantrik Terai Mukti Morcha (Jwalasingh)
21. Janatantrik Terai Mukti Morcha (Prithvi)
22. Janatantrik Terai Mukti Morcha (Rajan)
23. Janatantrik Terai Mukti Morcha (Visphot)
24. Khumbuwan Democratic Munch
25. Khumbuwan Democratic Munch
26. Khumbuwan Ladaku Dal
27. Kirant Janabadi Workers Party
28. Liberation Tiger of Terai Illam
29. Madhes Virus Killers Party
30. Madhes Silent Killers
31. Madhes Terai Munch
32. Madhes Krantikari Dal
33. Madhes Mukti Tigers
34. Madhes Rastra Janaktanti Party
35. Madhes Special Force
36. Madhes Rastra Janakranti Party (Krantikari)
37. Madhes Terai Mukti Morcha
38. Madhesi Mission Janakranti Terai Mukti Morcha
39. Madhesi Rastrya Janakranti Party
40. Madhesi Rastrya Janakranti Terai Mukti Morcha (Krantikari)
41. Madhesi Tigers
42. Mahan Madhes Krantikari Party
43. Mandhesi Janamukti Morcha
44. Mandhesi Liberation Tigers
45. Mongol Organisation
46. Mongolian Rebels

47. Nagraj
48. National Republican Party Nepal
49. National Terriorist Encounter committee
50. Nepal Defence Army
51. Nepal Ganatrantrik Young Tigers Group
52. Nepal Gorkha Army
53. Nepal Janakranti Party
54. Nepal Rebels' Group
55. Pallo Kirant Limbuwan Rastriya Munch
56. People's Army
57. Rastriya Janakranti Party
58. Rastriya Army Nepal
59. Rastriya Liberation Army
60. Revolutionary Left Wing
61. Royal Defence Army
62. Sanghiya Limbuwan Rajyaparishad (Kumar Langden)
63. Sanghiya Limbuwan Rajyaparishad (Misekhang)
64. Sanghiya Limbuwan Rajyaparishad (Sanjuhang Palungwa)
65. Sanghiya Ganatantrik Rastriya Morcha
66. Sanyukta Bidroha Morcha
67. Samyukta Janakranti (Anand)
68. Samyukta Janakranti Morcha
69. Samyukta Janakranti Terai Mukti Morcha
70. Samyukta Liberation Front of Nepal
71. Samyukta Tharu Mukti Morcha
72. Shahi Mukti Morcha
73. Shantika lagi Kranti Terai
74. Sudoor Paschim Kranti Dal
75. Tamang Cobra

76. Rastriya Mukti Sena
77. Rastriya Samanantar Jwalamukhi
78. Terai Army
79. Terai Bagi
80. Terai Commando
81. Terai Control Army
82. Terai Control Force
83. Terai Defence Army
84. Terai Ekata Parishad
85. Terai Encounter Party
86. Terai Jagaran Sangharshashil Morcha
87. Terai Janakranti Morcha
88. Terai Janakranti Party
89. Terai Janamukti Krantikari Party
90. Terai Janatantrik Mukti Morcha
91. Terai Kavre
92. Terai Liberation Force
93. Terai Madhes Mukti Tigers
94. Terai Madhesi Party
95. Terai Military Morcha
96. Terai Mukti Morcha
97. Terai Putra
98. Terai Rastriya Janakranti Party (Krantikari)
99. Terai Rastriya Mukti Sena
100. Terai Samyukta Janakranti Party
101. Terai Tigers
102. Tharu Rastriya Morcha Nepal
103. Ulfa Group
104. Utthan Sangh

105. Viral Killer
106. Vishan Himali Bagh
107. Aayam Bhumi Madhes Sarkar

NB: The total number presented here may have altered. They are very frequently merging and splitting. So, the number may frequently change. Among them, 29 are listed as the most active by Nepal Police. Ministry of Home Affairs has reported the 109 armed groups in total. Source: *Gorkhapatra*, 26 April 2009].

Annex 2: People who lost their lives during the Terai-Madhes uprising

S. N.	*Name*	*VDC/metropolitan*	*District*
1	Ramesh Kumar Mahato	Majahura	Siraha
2	Bechan Yadav	Dodhna	Siraha
3	Ramsworap Mehta	Inaruawa	Sunsari
4	Shyam sunder Mehta	Inaruawa	Sunsari
5	Hari Mehta	Inaruawa	Sunsari
6	Pramod Sada	Mahadeva	Siraha
7	Vijay sahani	Mahadeva	Siraha
8	Mohammad Mudacin	Charipatti	Siraha
9	Bhagati Mandal	Inaruawa	Sunsari
10	Nirmal Kumar Rajbangsi	Haatkhola	Morang
11	Shesh Abdul asaraf	Kalayai	Bara
12	Majid Mohammad Mansoor	Feta	Bara
13	Koili Kori	Puraina	Banke
14	Khodahe Godia	Puraina	Banke
15	Sadanand Yadav	Biratnagar	Morang
16	Rajkumar Kamat	Biratnagar	Morang
17	Mahabir Sah	Birgunj	Parsa
18	Dipendra Sah	Birgunj	Parsa
19	Rajesh Thakur	Parkauli	Mahottari
20	Kari Thakur	Janakpur	Dhanusha
21	Shiva Shankar Yadav	Dharapani	Dhanusha

22	Ashif Ali Mikrani	Malangawa	Sarlahi
23	Dinesh Ray Yadav	Gamharia	Sarlahi
24	Ram Ekwal Ray	Shiripur	Sarlahi
25	Sanjay Kumar Yadav	Jamunia	Sarlahi
26	Tallu Hasda Hemram	Haatkhola	Morang
27	Tularam Tripathy	Khajura	Banke
28	Kasiram Harijan	Belhari	Banke
29	Ram Narayan Sah	Salempur	Sarlahi

Source: Gautam (2008)

Annex 3: Agreement between the Government of Nepal and the Madhesi People's Right Forum, Nepal

As a continuation and realisation of the feelings of the historic people's movement of 2006/2007, and in order to end all aspects of discrimination against Madhesis, indigenous people/Janajatis, Dalits, women, backward classes and minorities, including the Muslim community, by the centralised and unitary government, and in order to restructure the state as an inclusive democracy and in a federal manner, so as to create an environment inclusive of Madhesis and all Nepalese people in the national mainstream, this agreement has been reached today between the Government of Nepal and the Madhesi People's Right Forum, Nepal.

1. To immediately implement the government's decision to honour all Madhesi activists killed during the movement and to provide compensation to their families.
2. To provide relief to those injured, blinded and disabled during the movement and to arrange for the immediate medical treatment of all injured people who are yet to receive treatment.
3. To annul all charges made against the leaders and workers of the Forum during the movement.
4. To ensure balanced proportional representation and partnership of Madhesis, indigenous people/Janajatis, Dalits, women, backward classes, disabled people, minority communities and Muslims who have been excluded for

generations, in all organs and levels of government and in power structures, mechanisms and resources.

5. To immediately establish a commission for state restructuring and ensure that it comprises of experts in an inclusive manner.
6. Arrangements will be made for a federal state with regional autonomy while the sovereignty, national unity and integrity of Nepal will be kept intact during the restructuring of the state. The rights, nature and limits of regional autonomy will be as decided by the Constituent Assembly.
7. To accord national recognition to the identity, language and culture of the Madhesis.
8. To have suitable proportional representation in all political appointments by the government, in foreign service and services including the education sector, as well as in commissions.
9. To give public holidays during all major Muslim festivals. To enact laws to protect the ethnicity, language, gender, religion, culture and traditions of Muslim people as well as the Madrassa Board.
10. To end all discrimination based on ethnicity, language, gender, religion, culture, national and social origin, political and other ideologies and guarantee human rights.
11. To establish a trilingual language policy for official work, education and international communication, including (a) mother tongue, (b) the Nepalese language and (c) English.
12. To solve the following Dalit-related problems:

a) Arrange for severe legal punishment for those who discriminate based on caste and practice untouchability.

b) Arrange for the effective implementation of a policy for free and compulsory education for Dalits, at least at the primary level.

c) Arrange for special opportunities and reservations in education and employment.

d) Arrange for homes for landless Dalits and alternate means of livelihood.

13. To solve problems related to citizenship by redeploying the Citizenship Distribution Teams to the villages for easy and accessible distribution of the citizenship certificates.

14. To adopt a balanced and just policy for the distribution of revenue and income generated from the Madhes and other rural regions.

15. To continue the process of returning and ensuring the return of houses, land and property seized by the CPN (Maoist) and also to expedite the return of weapons seized by them [CPN (M)] to their rightful owners.

16. To industrialise the country and increase industrial production, and to establish an Industrial Security Force to guarantee industrial security.

17. Both sides to stay committed to conducting the Constituent Assembly election in an impartial, peaceful and fear-free environment. In order to ensure the impartiality of the Constituent Assembly, necessary arrangements must be made to prevent the misuse of the current legislature-parliament including the mechanisms, resources and power of the state.

18. The Ministry of Information and Communication to appoint Madhesi media experts and journalists in all organs and levels of government-owned media, including TV, radio and print and to ensure inclusive proportional representation of Madhesis in the government communication commissions, bodies and delegations.

19. To create a search team to look for and conduct a special investigation into the abduction and disappearance of Jitendra Shah, the Chairman of the Madhesi Youth Forum in the Kathmandu valley, and to immediately make the situation public.

20. To immediately establish a High Level Task Force for Inclusion to determine the rules and draft laws necessary for

the inclusion of Madhesis, indigenous peoples/Janajatis, Dalits, women, etc. in all organs and levels of the state.

21. To guarantee the constitutional rights of ethnic, linguistic and religious minorities based on the principles of the United Nations and international human rights organisations on the rights of minorities.

22. To bring to an end the various movements being carried out by the Madhesi People's Rights Forum.

The Government of Nepal will immediately fulfil those agreements that can be fulfilled promptly and will fulfil other provisions in the course of time. A United Monitoring Mechanism will be established to carry out and oversee the implementation process and to periodically review the implementation.

[Signed]	[Signed]
Upendra Yadav	Ram Chandra Paudel
Coordinator	Coordinator
Madhesi People's Rights Forum	Nepal Government Talks Team

Date: 30 August 2007 (13 Bhadra 2064)

Note: While still demanding the establishment of a republic and a proportional electoral system, the Madhesi People's Right Forum, Nepal will give top priority to the Constituent Assembly elections, will participate in them and will continue its efforts to make them a success.

[Signed]

....

Upendra Yadav

Coordinator

Madheshi People's Right Forum, Nepal

Date: 30 August 2007 (13 Bhadau 2064)

Source: Unofficial translation from the original Nepali by UNMIN

Annex 4: Agreement between the Government of Nepal and the United Democratic Madhesi Front (UDMF)

Respecting the sentiments and aspirations of the Madhesi people of Nepal, expressed during the protests and movements that they have organised time and again for equal rights, this agreement was signed between the Government of Nepal and the United Democratic Madhesi Front, to ensure (the establishment of) a federal democratic republic in Nepal (with a) multiparty democratic system of governance, by guaranteeing equality, freedom and justice for all the nation's people, as well as by putting an end to all types of discrimination. This agreement will be immediately implemented. The points of the agreement are as follows.

1. The state shall declare as martyrs those who were killed during the Madhes movement and shall provide adequate compensation to those maimed and those who are yet to receive compensation. Similarly, arrangements shall be made for those injured during the movement to receive medical expenses and those martyred shall be given due recognition and their families shall be provided Rupees one million as relief, and those arrested shall be immediately released.
2. By accepting the Madhesi people's call for an autonomous Madhes and other people's desire for a federal structure with autonomous regions, Nepal shall become a federal democratic republic. In the federal structure, power shall be divided between the centre and states in a clear manner according to the (constitutional) list. The states shall be fully autonomous and shall enjoy full rights. By keeping Nepal's sovereignty and integrity intact, the decision regarding details of the (constitutional) list and the division of power between the centre and the states shall be made by the Constituent Assembly.
3. The existing legal provision for 20 percent, in Sub-section 14 of Section 7 of the Election of Members to the Constituent Assembly Act 2064, shall be changed to 30 percent.

4. It shall be mandatory for the state to carry out appointments, promotions and nominations in a manner such that there is inclusive proportional representation of Madhesis, indigenous nationalities, women, Dalits, (people from) backward regions and minority communities in all state bodies, including the security sector.
5. Proportional, inclusive and group entry [*tr.* entry in the army as a group] of Madhesis and other communities shall be ensured in order to give the Nepal Army a national and inclusive character.
6. The Government of Nepal and the United Democratic Madhesi Front request all armed groups agitating in the Terai to come to talks for a peaceful political process and to find a solution through dialogue. The Government of Nepal will take immediate steps to create a favourable environment for this purpose. We appeal to everyone to help conduct the Constituent Assembly election on 10 April in a peaceful, violence-free, impartial, fair and fear-free environment.
7. The Government of Nepal will immediately release all those who have been detained, withdraw cases filed against Madhesi leaders and party cadres of the Forum as well as of other parties, and immediately implement all other points of the 22-point Agreement signed between the Government of Nepal and the Madhesi People's Rights Forum on 30August 2007 (13 Bhadra 2064).
8. All the protest programmes called by the United Democratic Madhesi Forum shall be immediately withdrawn. The Government of Nepal will be responsible for the constitutional, legal, political and administrative aspects of the points of this agreement. The government shall form a high-level monitoring committee including members of the Front to monitor the implementation of this agreement.

Signatories to the Agreement:

- Rajendra Mahato, National Chairman, Nepal Sadvawana Party

- Upendra Yadav, Central Coordinator, MPRF
- Mahantha Thakur, Chairman, Terai-Madhes Democratic Party
- Girija Prasad Koirala, Prime Minister, Government of Nepal

28 February 2008 (2064 Falgun 16)

Source: Unofficial translation from the original Nepali, by United Nations Mission in Nepal (UNMIN)

Annex 5: Agreement between Chure Bhawar Ekta Samaj (CBES) and the Government of Nepal

The fourth phase of talks between the Talks Team of the Ministry of Peace and Reconstruction and Chure Bhawar Pradesh Ekta Samaj, Nepal was conducted on 13 September 2007 (27 Bhadra 2064) at the Ministry of Peace and Reconstruction in a cordial environment and the following agreements were reached upon:

1. Necessary legal steps will be taken to withdraw the cases against the nine activists (of Chure Bhawar Samaj), who were accused of murder and arrested during the Chure Bhawar movement in Yagyabhumi VDC of Dhanusa district. Also, other cases registered and arrest warrants made during the movement will be annulled.
2. Arrangements will be made immediately to provide people with services as protection issues have made it difficult to travel to (district) headquarters to utilise the services provided by the government bodies.
3. The government's decision to provide one million rupees to the family of Mangal Bahadur Gurmachhan, who received martyrdom after being killed by the police during the movement of Chure Bhawar Pradesh Ekta Samaj, should be implemented immediately. Arrangements should also be made to provide medical treatment to those who were injured during the movement and have still not received treatment, including the Vice Chairman of Chure Bhawar Pradesh Ekta Samaj.

4. The process of providing relief to the families of those who have been killed by the attacks of various armed groups in Terai should be continued.
5. The responsibility of investigating incidents that took place during the movement in Chure Bhawar region has been handed over to the commission formed to investigate Terai incidents. The Commission should be provided the support it needs to complete its work on time. On the basis of the report (presented by the Commission), appropriate action should be taken against those responsible for damages to life and property in the region, and relief should be provided to the people.
6. While restructuring the state, autonomous federal system should be established as determined by the Constituent Assembly, such that Nepal's sovereignty, national unity and integrity are strengthened.
7. Work related to development and forestry, and contract-based work of stone, sand, soil, gravel etc. in the Chure Bhawar region should be carried out only after agreements have been reached with the local bodies.
8. All sides should remain active in order to maintain mutual harmony and to develop mutual understandings between the people of Terai/Madhes, hill and mountain regions so that national unity and integrity can be strengthened.
9. Chure Bhawar Pradesh Ekta Samaj expresses its commitment to help conduct the upcoming Constituent election on 22 November in a free, fair and fear-free environment and withdraws all plans for the movement.

[Signed]	[Signed]
Ram Chandra Poudel	Keshab Prasad Mainali
Coordinator	Chairman
Nepal Government Talks Team	Chure Bhawar Pradesh Ekta Samaj

Date: 13 September 2007 [27 Bhadra 2064]

Source: Unofficial translation from the original Nepali by the United Nations Mission in Nepal (UNMIN)